The

TWEEN YEARS

A Parent's Guide for Surviving
Those Terrific, Turbulent, and Trying Times
Between Childhood and Adolescence

DONNA G. CORWIN

CB

CONTEMPORARY BOOKS

Library of Congress Cataloging-in-Publication Data

Corwin, Donna G.
    The tween years : a parent's guide for surviving those terrific,
turbulent, and trying times between childhood and adolescence /
Donna G. Corwin.
        p.   cm.
    ISBN 0-8092-2995-1
    1. Preteens.   2. Preteens—Psychology.   3. Child rearing.
4. Parenting.   I. Title.
HQ777.15.C67   1998
649'.12—dc21   98-6778
                                                                CIP

Cover photograph by Sharon Hoogstraten
Cover design by Monica Baziuk
Interior design by Jeanette Wojtyla

Published by Contemporary Books
A division of NTC/Contemporary Publishing Group, Inc.
4255 West Touhy Avenue, Lincolnwood (Chicago), Illinois 60646-1975 U.S.A.
Copyright © 1999 by Donna Corwin
Printed in the United States of America
International Standard Book Number: 0-8092-2995-1

98 99 00 01 02 03 QP 17 16 15 14 13 12 11 10 9 8 7 6 5 4 3

To Alexandra, my precious daughter.
You are my inspiration—
my turbulent and terrific Tween.

Contents

Acknowledgments

To STAN, my husband. Thank you for your love, support, and belief in me always, your brilliant sense of knowing where to knock, and your keen eye for what works.

To KARA, my editor and child rearing compatriot. You always listen and support my work 100 percent. Thank you.

To FAYE CORWIN for her wit, wisdom, and love.

To my friends and all of the parents who indulged my probing questions. Thanks for sharing so much of your lives with me.

A special thank-you to ALEX and all of her friends, especially Rena, Ali, Marisa, Julia, Molly, Erin, and Morgan, for their willingness to share their thoughts and feelings openly and honestly.

ANN, thank you for once again turning out a perfect manuscript. Your flying fingers did it again.

To CRAIG BOLT, thanks for your great work on the book.

Introduction

The Tween years are perhaps the most perplexing stage in your child's development. Not yet a teenager, certainly no longer a little tot, your developing child is as confused as you are about this awkward time. This is a time of discovery and change, and your child needs you to guide him through this in-between stage into adolescence.

Anyone who lives with a Tween will recognize the following profile. A Tween is part child, part teenager.

One minute she likes Barbie dolls, the next she is hiding them under her bed.

One minute he's playing cowboys and Indians, the next he's blasting rock music, watching MTV.

They slam their door shut, but then ask you to tuck them into bed.

She wants to wear crop tops and tight, black hip huggers, but she secretly loves her pink flowered pajamas.

He's too old for "regular dorky" clothes, and demands he wear shirts with names like Bilabong, Top Dawg, and Stussy.

Tweens think they know it all and are full of *attitude.* They'll kiss you in private, but never in public. And don't ask for "I love you's." They come when you least expect them.

Don't ever act like you know anything about your Tween because you'll quickly get shot down with that look that says, "You're uncool." Even if you were a hippie in the '60s and '70s, your input is not welcome. Your child will remind you that times have changed.

When I joined my daughter in singing a song by the Spice Girls, she abruptly stopped singing and looked at me like I had just insulted her. "Mommy," she asked, "what are you doing?" Well, I thought I was singing, but she insinuated that my musical interlude was a personal affront to her total being.

I have also been warned not to dress "too young," "talk too hip," or "hang out" with my daughter's friends. The fact that I was once young, hip, wore cool clothes, and listened to rock 'n' roll has no bearing on my daughter's feelings toward me.

She wants me in the background. Parents are symbols to their children, and no matter how much you may have been like your child, he wants his individual experience of growing up. He does not want his parents overidentifying with him. But, unlike teenagers, who become more self-sufficient as the years pass, Tweens have high parental expectations. My husband and I are expected to be our daughter's full-time chauffeur, endless money pit, video rental retriever, and general "give-me, get-me, take-me, do-for-me" machine. These are some of the "attitudes" that you will have to learn to deal with, or you are in for many years of Tween battles. Your Tween wants you close, but far away. You may sometimes be confused by what your role is.

Knowing that the Tween years are temporary, usually lasting from about age ten to thirteen, should give you great solace. I am willing to wait out these "in-between" years with grace and dignity. But I feel that it is best to be armed and ready with the necessary information about our wonderful and perplexing preteens. Raising a twelve-year-old places me right in the thick of the Tween years.

There are big changes taking place inside Tweens, and many of these changes need to be addressed. Tweens are testing to see how far they can push as they make the transition from one stage to another. They (and you) will be dealing with physical, social, and psychological changes. Parents should be prepared with concrete parenting tools to help their children solve specific problems and address their questions. This is what *The Tween Years* provides.

This book deals with commonsense approaches for a variety of situations such as: parent/child conflicts, how to reach and maintain good communication, early eating disorders, boy/girl behavior, hormonal changes, sensitive issues, how to teach your child responsibility, and problem solving. One of the most enlightening chapters in the book will be an open dialogue with Tweens (Chapter 10). Certainly the preteens themselves are the best ones to communicate to parents how they feel, what they believe, and where they see themselves in this complex society. Most parents will recognize their own child in the Tween Talk chapter, and probably gain enormous insight.

The Tween Years is a no-nonsense survival guide for parents that includes humorous personal stories, parent questions and answers, and psychologist interviews. I have compiled the vital information that every parent needs as their child enters this sometimes trying, sometimes turbulent, and certainly terrific stage called "the Tween years."

∼ 1 ∼

What's Happening to You—to Me— to Us?

When Bette Davis said in an old black and white movie, "Hold on tight. It's gonna be a bumpy ride . . . ," she could easily have been referring to adolescence—those years between ten and thirteen when parents and Tweens yell, cry, and tear at each other with frustration comparable to front-line battles—where the troops only retreat from death or exhaustion.

A Tween is a combination of the words *teen* and *in between*. Your Tween is in between childhood and the teenage years—a time of exploration, growth, change, and turbulence. Any time one is in between, he or she is squeezed in the middle, and no one likes being in this uncomfortable position.

The Tween years are not a time to take it easy. Parental input and guidance are vital during this time. The relationship, rules, boundaries, and communication you establish now will take you into the serious teenage years when a solid foundation can be your lifeline to your child.

During adolescence, emotions and hormones run amok. Parents, unprepared to cope with the fast and furious changes taking place in their Tweens, become reactive and often explosive. Their years of setting down rules, values, and expectations are suddenly challenged by the emerging Tween, who is questioning, experimenting, and searching to find an identity separate from his parents'. Learning to be understanding and sympathetic—to communicate and be open with your Tweenager, as opposed to being reactive, will help you establish a strong bond with your child. The closer your relationship, the more influence you will inevitably have and the chance of having your Tween respect your opinion.

Once we reach adulthood, our bodies, our minds, and our values are fairly stabilized. We move along on an even keel trying to deal with life as it happens. We know what kind of friends we want, what clothes look best on us, and how to handle adverse situations. We're more cautious, less impulsive, and certainly not as carefree. We look back at the traits of adolescence with envy: naiveté, fearlessness, curiosity, and the pursuit of fun, fun, and more fun. Yes!

It is the way these traits are manifested that causes so much conflict between parents and Tweenagers. Even if you experimented with "on the edge" things as a Tween, and even if you turned out just terrific, the overriding fear that maybe your Tween will not come through this period intact overrides your reason.

The attitudes of adults and preteens shift greatly as roles change. We want our Tweens to remain "children," but it's difficult to treat them as your children when they are wearing bras, playing spin the bottle, studying chemistry, and wearing *your* size-9 shoes.

Just the physical changes alone are monumental to a young preteen. A mother is no longer alone with premenstrual tension. There are at least two screaming banshees in the house. Boys' and girls' thoughts turn to each other and never turn away. There is a preoccupation with love and romance. Voices start to change, breasts grow, boys finally get taller, and moms' clothes fit their daughters.

When one mother admitted that her clingy daughter no longer asked her what to wear and didn't confide in her anymore, she was upset. Suddenly, mom saw her daughter in "weird" costumes, unlike anything she would have picked out. Her fashion advice was completely overlooked. Mom was out-of-date and out-of-style as far as this Tween was concerned.

Although she worried that her daughter was always too much of an extension of herself, she still found it hard to let go. Finally, adolescence gave her an opportunity to see her daughter establish her own opinions and ideas. Letting go of the controls was difficult for this mom. But seeing that her Tweenage daughter had the inner resources to become her own person was worth the letting go. Although this may seem like a trivial matter, it signifies a first step toward adolescent autonomy.

Accepting changes in your Tween will help you cope with this rite of passage when the problems really get tough. Try to understand that certain behaviors—like moodiness and disinterest in the family—are all part of the Tween passage. You may not like these new areas your Tween is exploring, but if you are willing to be supportive and strong, it will be a positive transition. If you are constantly angry and overcontrolling, you will truly be in for a bumpy ride.

The Emerging Intellect

Mike's twelve-year-old son, Ethan, proclaimed that he didn't like the President. Mike asked him, "Why?"

Ethan was perplexed. He merely answered, "Just because. I don't think he's good. My friend Jonathan said so."

Mike was upset. He challenged Ethan. He told him that if Ethan was going to venture his opinion about someone or something, he had to come up with a minimum of three valid and thought-out reasons why he felt the way he did, and saying his reason for his opinion was because his friend said so didn't count.

A Tween is filled with opinions about everything. His mind is becoming more inquisitive. Your Tween wants to know about complex subjects and is perturbed if you exclude him from adult conversation. He is at an age where he wants to be seen and heard. It is not enough for your Tween to merely state his opinion. He is adamant about what he says and often will go to great lengths to convince you that he is right. Often you will be surprised to find out that your Tween is versed in subjects you know nothing about, especially new technology and computers.

Family discussions about serious subjects—politics, religion, or relationships—can expand communication with your child. Don't be afraid to talk about subjects that might feel uncomfortable. It is better that your Tween discuss sensitive subjects with you than with his friends who might have incorrect or skewed visions of current events.

Encourage your child to read the paper and watch the news. Get him a subscription to *Time* or *Newsweek*. A child of eleven or twelve is not too young to become aware of the world's condition. Let your child know you are open to talking about *any* subject. If your Tween's opinion is based on what a friend said, challenge him (without backing him into a wall) and ask for examples and reasons why he formed his opinion. You can be a link to teaching your Tween critical, objective thinking. This is a crucial time for his emerging intellect. Your Tween will take great intellectual leaps over the next few years. The biggest problem with the Tween mind is that it is certain it knows more than yours, which brings us to the "no" years.

The "No" Years

This is an age that may seem like a repeat of the toddler years. Everything is "No!" There is a great deal of oppositional behavior and continual push/pull interaction with friends, family, and teachers. This behavior comes from the striking out for independence. Tweens want to make their mark—to assert who they are apart from their parents.

"I'm my own person!" said one eleven-year-old in an attempt to separate her ego from her mother's. The girl made such a statement to make it clear that she had her own ideas and aspirations. The mother, instead of fighting her daughter, can use this time as an opportunity to challenge, inform, and direct her daughter's ideas into a positive framework.

Ask your child questions. *Listen* attentively to what she has to say. *Explore* ideas together. Try to be more open-minded and realize that your Tween needs a bit of freedom. This "easing up" should come gradually between the ages of ten and thirteen, when the desire for more autonomy increases.

Tweens like to confront every issue. You can get worn down from arguing about even the most insignificant item. Tweens are "know-it-alls." They think their parents are old and stupid, so don't take any of this personally. They will contradict, talk back, and throw off attitude. Their once perfect parents no longer look so perfect. The Tween years start the time when your children are no longer as respectful of what you know. Don't push your knowledge onto your child—offer it, and don't be surprised if they refuse to accept it.

Like a toddler who is prone to temperamental outbursts, so is a Tween. Much of this temperament is hormone-driven. But don't be surprised if out of nowhere your preteen has a full scale temper tantrum. As you would behave with a toddler, don't get hooked in. Back off until the tantrum subsides. Confrontation will only exacerbate an already hot situation. Since everything is a "no" and a confrontation, it might be best to back off of unimportant topics.

A Loss

One evening I asked my twelve-year-old daughter if she wanted to play Scrabble® with me and her dad. She rolled her eyes, "Why?"

"Why? We're a family," I answered.

"I don't do that anymore, Mom. I'm not a little kid anymore."

I didn't know that an evening of Scrabble signaled that she was a little girl. But her interests were no longer family directed. Her friends had suddenly taken precedence over us. Actually, the phone and the computer had taken center stage over Mom and Dad.

I wanted my cuddly girl back, the one who thought that everything I said was wonderful. She clung to my words, listening intently. Now my words were useless. She nodded when I spoke, but there was a blank stare on her face. Words were suddenly lost on my Tween. If you want your Tween to respond to you, go for the shock effect. Make your words count. When you speak, your preteen should know you are serious. Otherwise, your words will be lost.

The Tween years may feel like you have also lost your child. To be pushed aside may be hurtful, but it is normal and age-appropriate. You need to be able to let go of your preteen but retain parental control. It's a balancing act that will call to task your parenting skills and a great deal of patience. Your child needs and wants you as his anchor. You represent unconditional love and acceptance at a fickle and changeable time in his life. You may feel hurt and sad during this period.

This is not really a time of loss. It is a new phase of development for your child. Watch, nurture, guide, and enjoy the changes taking place. Appreciate the human being into which your child is developing. You are not losing a child—you are gaining a new, interesting, and exciting young person.

～ 2 ～

Physical Milestones

Big Changes Ahead

It is difficult to imagine your son wearing the same size shoe as you or shaving fresh stubble. Can you fathom your daughter wearing a bra, waxing her legs, and using tampons? After all, these are your babies. You changed her diaper, dressed him in overalls, fed him cereal, and wiped her tears away.

Once the Tweens are upon you, the physical changes in your child are enormous. Your son will likely be able to run circles around Dad on the basketball court. Your daughter will start looking more like Mom with rounder hips and developing breasts. Shopping for clothes will become an ordeal. Be prepared for your daughter to try on dozens of outfits and then tell you, "I have nothing to wear!" or

"Nothing fits right!" She'll go into Mom's closet looking for baggy jeans and old shirts. The hours will tick away while she decides what to put on.

Milestones is the appropriate word for the changes your child will go through in the next phase of development—from child to preteen is an enormous leap. My friend Jill remarked how odd it was to see the girls tower above the boys during her son's fifth grade spring music festival. They were not only taller, but some of the girls looked like sexy teenagers with developing bodies. But when the girls smiled, it was a sea of shining metal. The boys looked chubby or puny. There wasn't a hunk in sight. That sums up the beginning of puberty.

By ten, some girls are beginning to develop small breast buds, while boys are barely developing muscles. The growth phase for boys comes at about age fourteen. Usually boys will develop underarm hair at about age twelve, but not much else is growing. This in-between time is marked by awkward physical changes. Your child might develop minor acne, gain weight, and need braces on her teeth. Your daughter might want pierced ears and short cropped hair like a bald eagle. Your son might want to wear oversized clothes and shave his hair. Your once gorgeous children might suddenly appear gawky or funny looking.

During their developing years, girls become totally preoccupied with their bodies and everyone else's. An enormous amount of time is spent making comparisons to other girls—who have breasts, whose are bigger, who shaves her legs, who has hair "down there," and who got her period. Your child might be worried if she is delayed or advanced in her development, so reassure her that she's normal. Her curiosity might be mixed with embarrassment, and your Tween's hunched-over body posture will reveal her newfound discomfort with her body. Many Tween girls walk hunched over in an effort to hide their developing chests.

Boys are less embarrassed—and more preoccupied with sexy books, magazines, and dirty jokes. The more sophisticated boys might be aware of how some girls move and will make comments like, "She has great legs" or "Check out that hot body." This is innocent and normal. But make sure your son is versed on how to treat a girl. Emphasize respect and sensitivity. How a preteen boy acts toward a girl now will influence his attitude toward women for the rest of his life.

Physical changes are the biggest turning point for Tweens. Once they start to look more mature, you may be fooled into thinking that they *are* more mature. A Tween is still young—and prone to silly and foolish behavior. Don't be surprised if your fully developed twelve-year-old daughter wants to jump rope or play with the younger kids. The mind does not always develop as quickly as the body. For this reason, parents are often annoyed when a Tween is so immature and sloppy. The full process of physical and mental development takes quite a few years. Be understanding and sensitive during this awkward physical transition time.

Whatever you do, resist the urge to criticize his appearance. This is a physically awkward time for your child, and he needs your support and reassurance. Your Tween probably will be very self-conscious about his or her looks. It is best to emphasize healthy eating and good hygiene. With emerging puberty comes body odor and embarrassing situations. Help your child be prepared with the proper skin care preparations, deodorants, and feminine hygiene products. Acne can flare up and cause extreme mental stress for young preteens. Girls especially obsess about their skin. If your child does break out badly, take him to a dermatologist early on.

Be open and direct with your child. Let her know that you are there to talk about anything and answer any questions that she may ask. If you act embarrassed or disgusted, your child may feel like something is wrong or unnatural with him.

Period!

One mother going through early menopause at the same time that her eleven-year-old began to menstruate confessed that their house was like a hormonal explosion chamber. There was always someone cranky, moody, crying, or depressed. It was a strain on the nerves, especially for the mom who was trying to deal with her daughter's moods as well as her own.

This brings me to the highly sensitive subject of menstruating—"period," "curse," "the rag." Whatever you call it, it causes a lot of discomfort literally and figuratively for young girls.

Females can start to menstruate as early as nine or as late as fourteen or even fifteen. For this reason, a girl's body goes through a myriad of changes: breasts and pubic hair grow, her body fills out, and her skin can break out. If she gets her period early, she feels set apart from the other girls. Why our society is so skittish about such a natural physical process is perplexing. That's why it is the parent's, primarily the mother's, job to be informative, prepared, and understanding with her daughter.

You should talk with your daughter about why she menstruates, what physical changes her body goes through, and the symptoms her body will feel. Some girls get horrible cramps, so you might need to be prepared with Midol® and a hot-water bottle. Discuss the tension and mood changes that come with her period. But most important, let her know that her body is going through a natural monthly cycle and that the pain and discomfort are normal.

Physical changes lead to emotional changes. Learning to cope and helping your child cope during this stage are essential.

~ 3 ~

Emotions on the Run

There are many obstacles you will have to face with your Tween. The old saying, "Bigger kids, bigger problems," is a truism. The relationship you establish in these early adolescent years can help you greatly as you move into the more challenging teen years. It is vital to reassess your values and priorities with your child. A child's personality will be greatly influenced by the way the family interacts. It is important not to allow your Tween's "I could care less" attitude throw you off. Stay goal-oriented with your child, not child-centered. An example of this is the mother who suddenly saw her very mature eleven-year-old as a mini adult. This mom started allowing her child to make decisions that she was clearly not ready to make. In turn, the child became angry with her mom because she really didn't want to be treated like an adult. Neither the child nor the mom knew what to do with this new phase. The pendulum will swing daily between childhood and preadolescence, and you are best to stay balanced in the middle.

One minute your Tween might be asking you what French kissing is, and the next minute she might be wanting to sleep with her "blankie" because she is afraid of the dark. Try not to become shocked, angry, or judgmental. This "ying yang" behavior is age-appropriate. Tweens are prone to emotional highs and lows. Part of this is hormonal, part age-related.

Attitude

When your child turns about ten, you will notice something different. He has suddenly developed *attitude*. Attitude, for our purposes, is defined as the way we react to things or events. Tween attitude can be more intense than teen attitude at times because Tweens don't possess the emotional maturity and sensitivity that a sixteen- or seventeen-year-old may have.

For your purposes, think of attitude as reliving toddlerhood, but now your child is bigger and smarter. A perfectly adorable child can suddenly "go insane" if she forgets her science book before the final. A darling little boy now becomes explosive if you try to kiss him in public.

Your child now views you as an alien being. No matter how hip you may think you are, he thinks that you know nothing. And don't even try to wear anything sexy or too stylish, or your Tween will surely let you know she doesn't approve. You somehow have become a source of embarrassment. Do not take this rejection too personally. It is normal behavior. On the other hand, don't allow your Tween to negate you. You've lived longer, seen, done, heard, and experienced life. Your Tween is just beginning his journey and could learn and will learn a great deal from you.

Attitude is part hormonal changes, part preteen early rebellion, and part maturation. For the parent, it is part confusion, part frustration, and part wanting to throw your precious child out the window. But being the good parent that you are, you want to try and make sense of this new "Don't bug me, Mom," "I know that," and "I don't have to" behavior. Many parents of thirteen-year-olds have told me that their precious, well-behaved children are turning into obnoxious, big-mouthed preteens. Welcome to the club!

This newfound attitude begins with an awakening of the *self* of your child. Suddenly, he is given more responsibility and choices. He feels a stronger sense of mastery over situations, and mentally he has an awareness of the world around him. This time of awareness is marked by peer influence. This is a vital time for parents to really be aware of who this child plays with and what kind of influence his friends have on him.

Although your child has modeled your behavior from infancy, this shifts as he becomes a teenager. He starts to transfer his modeling behavior and emulate his friends as well as role models like celebrity sports figures and rock singers.

This modeling is usually nothing to worry about unless your child has taken it to the extreme. Some children are highly impressionable and react literally to what they see and hear. That is why it is important to monitor your child's choices of film, television, and music. One child may see a violent horror film and have no reaction. Another may have nightmares for years.

There are two schools of thought about how to deal with "attitude." One is to parent by punishing the child, and the other is to let natural consequences punish—teach a lesson. Assessing the situation and using both at the appropriate times is probably the best way to deal with Tween attitude. Whatever you do, try not to push your child away. Let him know that he is loved and cared about unconditionally, but you will not tolerate rude and disrespectful behavior.

Back Talk

"I never talked to my mother and father the way my thirteen-year-old mouths off at me," complained a weary mother. "If I did, my mom would have cracked me a good one."

This scenario was played out over and over for parents of the Baby Boom Generation. But it does not apply to today's kids. Crack a kid a good one and you might end up in court. We no longer have the ethic of hitting and slapping to silence our children. Some states consider hitting child abuse. Kids "mouth off" because they feel the freedom of expressing their emerging selves without the same fears we had of our parents. Perhaps the message of "express your feelings" has carried over too far and too literally in today's society.

There must be limits on what your child can and cannot say to you, and how far you will let him go. The words, the tone, and the attitude are all important when assessing whether your Tween is letting out healthy frustration or just being disrespectful and in need of discipline.

All of the parents I spoke with readily expressed frustration at their child's back talk. Quite frankly, a little fear never hurt a child.

It is best not to wait and take action down the line when your child mouths off. The first time he crosses the line, stop him cold in his tracks. Let him know he is *never* allowed to talk to anyone (let alone his parents) with that tone of voice and nasty attitude. If it happens a second time, immediately ground him or take away his privileges.

Modeling the behavior you would like your child to emulate is vital to showing him how to talk. If you yell, swear, and act nasty to him or others, he will mirror back your actions. Be firm, but try not to "lose it" when talking to your Tween. I know this can be difficult at times. Tweens can push you into a state of hysteria. Even if you do lose it, don't feel like all is lost. Sit down with your child; explain your sense of frustration over his actions. Let him know that parents are human and sometimes act out their anger inappropriately. But that does not excuse your child's behavior. He is to follow the rules set down by you and show respect.

The Flip Side

The flip side of attitude for a Tween is seen when there is truly a need in the family. Amy's twelve-year-old son, who gave her continual angst, was an incredible source of love and strength to her after she developed breast cancer and had to have a mastectomy.

"He couldn't help me enough," Amy confessed. "He knew this was serious, and a new maturity came into play. He set the preteen side of himself aside and focused positive attention on me for once."

Tweens really need you, even though they act like they don't. These sensitive years call for gentle guidance and a willingness to be flexible.

There is a kind of ying yang to Tweens. Just like when they were toddlers yearning to seek autonomy from Mom and Dad but needing a safe place to run to, the Tween displays much of this same behavior. The Tween needs a certain amount of freedom, but also needs a strong family to run to. You will be surprised when things really get rough for you or a family member how warm and caring your Tween can be.

Competition

The competition starts to heat up when your child hits ten. You'll notice a push to be the best athlete, the top student, the prettiest girl, or the funniest kid in class. Kids become conscious of their looks and are overly aware of their physical image. It may be difficult to convince your twelve-year-old daughter that the way a boy looks is only a minor part of his character. Give the lectures, and then let it go. Kids will "get it" later on when it counts. Right now, being smart or funny or kind is a sideline to good looks.

What is important is not to get caught up in comparisons. Judy had a habit of comparing her daughter, Lily, to other girls.

"Sophie gets better grades than you. Does she study more?" Judy would ask Lily.

"Megan wears her hair in a cuter style than your long, stringy hair. Catherine is such a great soccer player. You could be better if you worked on your kicking like Catherine does."

Lily felt defeated before she began. Her sense of self-worth was diminished. Why bother trying to do anything? She believed her mom didn't think she was "good enough" the way she was. She was sure that if she got an "A," her mom would complain why didn't she get an "A+" like Sue. If she made a goal in soccer, Lily thought her mom would say, "That's good, but you could have scored higher."

Competition is tough for a Tween who is being compared socially, academically, and athletically to everyone else. Your child is at an age where he might feel less empowered in certain areas, and if you aren't supportive, his self-esteem can be bruised. Competition heats up in the Tween years. Peer interaction is strong. Boys and girls are being noticed by one another, and the competition for who likes whom is big.

There is such a thing as healthy competition, wherein a Tween is competing against his personal best, another team, or a school standard. Unhealthy competition is when boys and girls vie for the "best." When Maggie heard her daughter's friends debating who was the most popular on a scale of one to ten, Maggie became concerned. They were rating best eyes, best legs, best smiles, best hair, and so on.

"Everything was being rated on a physical basis," said Maggie. "No one seemed interested in 'best' brains, best sense of humor, or most creative."

Maggie is in for an awakening. No matter how open-minded and equitable a parent teaches his child to be, chances are that Tween competition will be based on physical characteristics until your child matures. Think of this time as the age of discovery—where your child is discovering herself, the opposite sex, her new physical appearance, and a whole host of things. This age of physical discovery naturally causes a Tween to focus on and compete with others. This behavior is normal for this age group. If the competition becomes obsessive or mean, then it needs to be addressed.

This type of attitude is only damaging to the frail egos of Tweens. They are highly sensitive at this time and struggling with self-image and identity.

How to Stimulate Healthy Competition

- Emphasize your child's personal best.
- Don't make comparisons to siblings or friends.
- Use positive reinforcement for small efforts.
- Discuss the competitive edge that comes with hard work and dedication.
- De-emphasize competing for looks or material objects.
- An "I'm in your corner" attitude is so much healthier for your preteen's psyche.

When your child truly feels that you are in her corner, she will confide in you more and be willing to share her successes as well as failures without recrimination.

Expectations and Reinforcement

The chances of your child disappointing you are great. People will make mistakes and show their vulnerabilities. It is part of our nature. You need to see your child as imperfect in order to find and accept all that is good about him. Build his self-esteem with positive reinforcement, and by doing so you will inevitably encourage your child to improve and be the best that he can be. Showing your disappointment in your child causes him to feel not only discouraged, but he may think, "I'm never good enough for my parents. Why should I try?" If you expect too much, then you have nowhere to go.

Preteens are ultrasensitive, and their psyches need to be massaged. They backfire with the most innocent comment. When talking to your child, use positive statements that show your support of him.

The chart on page 28 will give you an idea of how to respond to your Tween without creating an angry response.

It is vitally important not to negate your child's feelings. It may seem ridiculous to you because your Tween is hysterical over a lost homework assignment or a pimple, but your child sees these things as *big* problems. She needs your understanding. Do not be

Positive-Negative Response Chart	
Positive	Negative
"I know you tried your best."	"You did terrible on that test."
"You'll do better next time."	"Why bother? You'll probably fail."
"You are terrific!"	"You're a loser."
"You seem to be troubled. Can I help?"	"What's the problem now? Stop complaining."
"That must make you feel bad."	"Don't feel that way."

condescending. Try to remember how you felt when you were a preteen. Sometimes your child needs you to just listen. Not every conversation necessitates a therapy-style session, and not every problem is yours to work out. Preteens need to start dealing with their own problems without parental involvement.

Not Fitting In

Kids begin to jockey for position around the age of nine or ten. Like adults, labels get pinned on certain children—the nerd, the "leader," the pretty one, the pushy one, the talker. These labels, which can serve them well as adults, may cause them trouble as children. As they become Tweens, it may be difficult to lose these labels. Preteens use labels to group other kids because it is easier to gain position and secure friends.

Most kids are eager to conform because they want acceptance, and looking or acting differently is not always in their social best interest. The questions for the parent are, do you encourage independence and uniqueness, or do you push your child toward more conformity and less social and emotional turmoil?

Actually, a little of both is what can help balance a child. It is imperative that children establish good self-esteem; therefore, feeling inner strength from his or her unique and different qualities. But no child wants to be a social outcast, and sometimes parents can guide their kids toward more socially acceptable behavior.

Self-esteem is perhaps the most important self-value a child can possess. With a good self-image, a person can accomplish so much more than someone who is unsure of himself, insecure, and self-hating. Liking yourself is the first step toward being a successful human being.

What's most important in preparing your child

for positive social interaction is making sure he has a good self-image.

Encouragement

Encouragement improves relationships between parents and children, increases the cooperation in the family, and helps children develop confidence, self-reliance, and the ability to face challenges.

- **Encouragement** is the process of focusing on an individual's resources in order to build that person's self-esteem and self-confidence. People who encourage are able to see what is positive in any interaction.
- **Self-encouragement** involves building a positive relationship with yourself, using self-valuing statements, and changing your discouraging beliefs.
- The **courage** to be imperfect allows you to take chances and make mistakes.

The skills of encouraging include:

- Listening
- Responding to feelings
- Focusing on strengths, efforts, and contributions
- Seeing alternatives
- Using humor

Encouragement is different from praise because encouragement focuses on a child's internal evaluation, recognizes any effort or improvement, and builds a child's ability to manage his own behavior positively. Encouraging words show support without making a value judgment.

During this turbulent and emotional time, it is vital to both give encouragement to your Tween and help him build self-esteem. He'll need it for the even more challenging years ahead when his values and sense of self may be called to task. The courage for a child to say "no" to drugs, early sexual experiences, and any number of teen challenges will take serious guidance, teaching, and positive reinforcement on your part.

Building Self-Esteem

Jillian declared, "I'm miserable. Nothing is good. I broke out. My braces hurt. My friend is mad at me, and I'm fat!"

Her worried parents didn't know what to do.

Tweens are emotional wrecks. They stare in the mirror first with love and then with hate. Their changing minds and bodies leave them with little self-esteem as puberty takes over like some alien being invading their persons.

For this reason, Tweens need a boost of encouragement from their parents. Encouragement focuses on everything positive in your child. This inevitably will boost his self-esteem. More important, your child needs to build inner confidence, so he doesn't solely rely on encouragement from you.

Self-esteem is one's inner confidence and how one feels about oneself. Positive self-esteem allows you to feel good about yourself. Encouragement rather than criticism will support your child and help him to trust your judgment and his own. In order to build self-esteem, you need to let your child know he doesn't have to be perfect.

The willingness to be imperfect is what forms good character. Being willing to admit your mistakes helps you and your child learn together. Encourage your child to take chances. Let him fail or fall and pick himself up. Tell him you are there to help, to teach, to listen, to respond, and to find alternatives. Help your Tween solve the problem. This will be useful for his entire life. Knowing how to problem-solve at an early age can help your child with society, school, and even more serious experiences as he matures.

Encouragement Tips

- Steer your child into activities that make him feel good.
- Reinforce your child's positive traits.
- Do not be critical—be constructive.
- Plan fun family activities.
- Encourage your child to invite friends over.
- Emphasize good values like friends, community service, intellectual activities, and religious activities.
- De-emphasize how your child looks, how much she weighs, and what she doesn't know.
- Never compare your child to other children.
- Acknowledge your child's feelings, but don't judge them.

Parenting Myths

- I have to control my child.
- My child has to love me always.
- I know what is best for my child.
- My child has to do well, or it reflects poorly on me.
- My child can never challenge my authority.
- I must be a perfect parent for my child.
- I can't show my feelings or I will look like a weakling to my child.

Tween Myths

- I have to be perfect in order for people to like me.
- If I do poorly, my parents will be disappointed in me.
- I have to be good-looking or I won't be popular.
- I must be a good athlete.
- I have to be thin.

The emotional life of a Tween is the core to his being. This stage will take you, as a parent, on an emotional roller coaster with him. You will be challenged to be consistent, which is difficult at this age. The Dr. Jekyll and Mr. Hyde nature of your Tween will require you to use all of your parenting skills—and then some. The next chapter will give you some idea of the school and social life of Tweens and how to help them be successful.

~ 4 ~

School and Social Success

The social life of a Tween is a dizzy and bumpy ride. It can go from elation to devastation in a matter of minutes. Tweens want friends and acceptance, but often don't know how to get them. It is the years when kids start to feel emotional pain over the smallest issue. Your child will have a best friend one day, and the next day declare her friend a mortal enemy. The path to mature socialization is paved with many lessons.

Social Power

Do you remember your social life at age ten, eleven, or twelve years old? Chances are, even if you were popular, you felt weird, ugly, and creepy half the time. The social highs and lows of Tween life vacillate greatly. Unfortunately, most children at this age do not have "developed" social skills and may be ostracized for their awkwardness. Parents often are angry because their children are not part of "the supposed in group," but pushing your child into being accepted can lead to trouble. He may choose an inappropriate group of friends. Helping your child develop social skills does not mean getting overly involved with his friends and problems. The best skill you can give him is to let him learn to work out his problems by himself. You will become his guide in making good choices.

Perhaps the best way to help your child find friends is to encourage his involvement in activities that he enjoys like sports, dance, drama, science club, and music where he can meet other kids who have similar interests. Many of these activities will help your child learn teamwork and cooperation.

Make your child feel comfortable by inviting his new friends over to your home. Help him be a good host. Hopefully his friends will reciprocate. Make your child aware of his expected behavior at a friend's home. Emphasize his use of "please," "thank you," and "may I." Reward his behavior, especially if another parent remarks about how well he behaved.

Back Off

Overinvolvement in your child's social life can get you into big trouble. First of all, your Tween does not want you involved. Secondly, you shouldn't be involved. Because of the fickle nature of Tweens, you will find your advice being disregarded. For instance, let's say you tell your child, "Don't play with Nancy if she's mean to you." There is every possibility that Nancy will be your daughter's best friend again the next day. Remember the ying yang of Tweens? You need to assess when it is appropriate to intervene in your child's social life.

There is nothing wrong with asking questions about your Tween's friends. You also need to know when to back off. Do not probe into private areas that might embarrass your child or invade her privacy, especially snooping through diaries and Internet mail. This is only—and I repeat *only*—OK if you suspect your child is using drugs or engaging in dangerous or inappropriate behavior. Show interest in the friends' parents. Information about the parents will tell you a lot about your child's friend.

The only time when you should intervene in your child's choice of friends directly is when the friend is clearly influencing your child in a negative way. It is important to set up rules ahead of time so

37

that your child will be able to have guidelines about his choice of friends.

It is also vital that you meet all of your child's friends. Encourage your child to invite his friends to your home for a play date or slumber party. Make sure you encourage your Tween to make his friends aware of the rules in your home. Be firm and consistent about your rules. By instilling a sense of pride and ownership in your child, he will be apt to be respectful of his home and personal things.

School Power

"Use your brain!" said one father to his twelve-year-old son who was perplexed by a science question. The father felt certain his son could find the answer with some thinking and exploring.

Independent thinking is one of the main areas that separates Tweens from younger children. Now that your Tween is older, he will be required to use his brain power in different ways. He will need to learn time management skills, independent study skills, how to work in group projects, and how to do long-term assignments. Your child will be expected to act independently and responsibly in a number of areas. He will have to maintain his locker, take on larger jobs in school, participate in middle school intramural athletics, and learn to interact with seven different teachers' personalities in one day.

The junior high school transition for Tweens can be overwhelming. They need parental support but not always too much parent involvement. You have to walk a fine line. Organization is a key to success during this transitional time. Homework, reports, tests, reading, and research all have to get done by designated dates. Many Tweens are disorganized and unable to meet deadlines on time, or they stay up until all hours of the night trying to finish a project. Time management can make a difference in school success. You can work on the following time management skills with your child.

Time Management

- Set up a schedule. A schedule, although not always followed to the minute, will help establish a *routine* for your Tween. Routines are important for keeping your child *on track* and organized.
- Make time for long-term projects and reports in your schedule. For instance, if a teacher gives a report due date of two weeks, then schedule 20 to 30 minutes a night to work on it.

Sample Time-Management Chart

Time	Monday	Tuesday	Wednesday	Thursday	Friday	Saturday	Sunday
3:00	Soccer		Soccer			Sports	
3:30		Snack				Sports	
4:30	Snack	Homework	Snack			Sports	
5:00	Homework	Homework	Homework			Sports	
6:30	Long-term projects	Homework	Homework		Sports		Work on projects if due
7:00	Dinner	Dinner	Dinner	Dinner	Dinner	Dinner	Dinner
8:00	Bath, Relaxation					Fun	Reading

School Study Skills
Your Tween Should Master

- Note taking
- Reading for comprehension
- Outlining skills
- Learning how to do research for projects
- Knowing how to study for a test by breaking up each section and studying a little at a time. Focus on what you don't know. Test yourself.
- Critical thinking skills (evaluating material and being able to discuss and give opinions about it)
- Mastering the multi-paragraph paper and how to construct and write a research paper
- Proofreading
- Test taking

Homework

Jill was looking through her eleven-year-old son's notebook when Josh burst through the door as if he had caught her stealing.

"What are you doing?" he questioned her.

Jill, feeling embarrassed and not understanding why, replied, "I'm checking your homework."

Josh was miffed. He let his mother know that he was old enough to do his own homework. Period.

Jill wasn't sure she should let her son do his homework on his own considering Josh was struggling in math. But then his other grades were fine. Jill was having trouble letting go, and it is easy to understand why. Parents are encouraged to help their children with homework. But by the time your child is a Tween, he needs to learn to work on his own. He needs to feel self-empowerment—that he is capable of successfully completing a task.

What you can do as a parent is instill good work habits that lead to better grades. The following guidelines should be used to help your child stay focused and positive.

Positive School Work Exchange

- All homework must be done before play, TV, or any other activity.
- Your child should have an organizer and plenty of supplies—paper, pencils, erasers, ruler, tape, glue, etc.
- Provide necessary books—dictionary, thesaurus, and an encyclopedia.
- Get your child a library card.
- Help your child be computer literate.
- Read to and with your child every day.
- Your child should have a place to do his work, preferably his own desk in his room.

Negative School Work Exchange

- Do not do your child's homework for him.
- Do not criticize your child's work.
- Do not overemphasize grades.
- Don't make comparisons between your child and his friends or siblings.
- Don't let school problems get overlooked and think they will disappear.

Approach your Tween with the attitude, "I am always here to help you with your work. If I don't know the answer, we'll find someone who does." This leaves the door open without *pushing* it open. When you exchange a positive attitude, your Tween will come to you—even if you don't have all the answers!

Parent-Teacher Bonding

No matter how old your child gets, it is important to maintain an ongoing relationship with his teacher. The teacher-parent bond can make a huge difference in your child's success. This is important in the Tween years because your child starts to pull away and does not communicate with you as to what is happening at school. Then you see a report card, and your mouth drops open from shock.

Keep the communication lines open with conferences, phone calls, and periodic notes. Usually the teacher welcomes parent action when a child is having trouble, but you want to get in there *before* there is trouble.

There are some effective strategies to create a parent-teacher bond. The first is a "start-of-school" note. At the beginning of the school year, write a note to the teacher letting her know that you are available to work in the classroom, and make time to do so. Ask that the teacher inform you of any problems (academic or behavioral) that occur in school. Get any books or materials your child needs and ask the teacher for additional reference books. Be your child's advocate. Take a positive perspective. Point out your child's best qualities and work to enhance his weak areas. Listen to his teacher, and don't become defensive.

If there is an ongoing problem that is affecting your child's school performance, then use a behavioral technique that works well with younger elementary school children—the "teacher-parent report." This report is like a daily report card that monitors your child's work for a short period of time. This works best with fourth, fifth, and sixth graders. It allows the parent to keep close tabs on their child's work and behavior. You can send the

Parent-Teacher Daily Report		
	School Work	Behavior
Poor		
Good		
Excellent		
Comments	*Example:* Completed assignments on time.	

teacher a stack of 3″ × 5″ cards with categories written on them. The teacher will check off the appropriate box, and the parent will act accordingly.

These notes will pinpoint behaviors and help you to get your Tween back on track. Certainly they will avoid the shocked, "Oh, I had no idea!" look when report card time rolls around.

Socialization Skills

The following socialization issues should be discussed with your Tween as a way to make friends:

- **Trust.** Remind your preteen that if she breaks a confidence, she breaks the "Golden Rule" of friendship, and her friend may not confide in her any longer.
- **Discriminate.** Don't tell everyone your problems. Tweens love to talk, and gossip can go round in circles and change drastically.
- **Don't tattle** unless it is a *serious* situation—for instance, if a friend is taking drugs or stealing.
- **Be fair** by learning to take turns and letting others go first. Tweens are notoriously all about "me."
- **Be independent.** Don't be afraid to express your thoughts and feelings.
- **Give in** once in a while. Sometimes it doesn't pay to argue about a silly matter. If it is really a big issue, then stick to your convictions.
- **Be your own person.** You don't have to follow the crowd. You can be the leader and trendsetter. Don't let someone else tell you if you are cool or not.
- **Take everything in moderation.** Pierced ears and not pierced noses, a streak of color in your hair and not multicolored layers, a fake fun tattoo or henna (it fades), not *permanent* (for life) markings on your body.
- **Avoid jealousy.** Be happy for others' successes and good traits, and you will be rewarded. Jeal-

ousy is a road to unhappiness, and ultimately you will lose friends.

Social power is about acceptance, sharing, and understanding. These are big concepts for preteens, especially at a time of conformity. But if you discuss what it means to be a good friend and model that behavior with your own friends, you will be bestowing an invaluable gift on your child.

~ 5 ~

Battle Stations

Anger

"Drop dead." "I hate you." "You don't understand me." "Leave me alone." "Follow my rules or leave." "I run this family, not you!" If you think these are the rantings of a bratty child or an abusive parent, you might just be wrong. This is the diatribe between a preadolescent, trying to be a contrary Tween, and a frustrated parent who is unable to cope with his preadolescent.

The anger that permeates parent-Tween conflicts cuts deeply and often leaves scars. Parents are suddenly thrust into new roles, and their Tweens may seem to be out-of-control—or rather out-of-their-control. Many parents, unprepared to cope with adolescence, use angry confrontation as their only resource to discipline their children. But anger only leads to more anger, and the parent-adolescent relationship can deteriorate into one of constant battles.

Anger escalates quickly with a Tween, and it often comes in the form of a smart-mouthed, nasty reply. Shocked and furious parents lash out with similar threat, anger, and discipline. There are a few children who get through childhood and adolescence like perfect angels, but I'd venture a bet that if you are reading this, your child is not in the angel category.

Anger is heightened, especially with girls, during the Tween years. Hormones and social problems become all important. You might even find yourself in a situation where your child says, "My friend knows more than you." Tweens really think their parents are clueless. When you stamp your feet and say "No!" to your Tween, he might come back with a retort like "Why?" The old "because I said so" may not work. As children get older, they start to reason and use clever manipulation. This can lead to arguing and negative interaction.

How to Control Anger

No matter how much control you have over your anger with others, you are almost guaranteed to lose your temper and become angry at your Tween more often than you ever thought imaginable. It is almost certain that your Tween will do or say something that will really push your buttons. The key is to recognize in advance what situations cause you to lose control. Then, devise a plan to prevent or greatly turn down the volume of your anger.

When you find yourself becoming continually angry with your Tween, it is essential to go through these four steps to assess what is really pushing your buttons:

Step 1: Recognize that it is normal age-appropriate behavior for your Tween to do or say something that will upset you. Expect it, and you will not be taken by surprise in the future.

Step 2: Define what specifically your Tween does that causes you to become angry. "Attitude" is too general a term to be useful. Be specific. What is it exactly that she does (e.g., talks back to you or lies about homework) that sets you off on the road to uncontrollable anger?

Step 3: If you view your child's actions as a direct threat to your authority as a parent, or as a defiant act simply to "get to you," then you are more likely to react with greater emotional intensity than if you view his behavior as the normal strivings for independence. Your mind-set regarding your adolescent's behavior has a lot to do with how you react.

Step 4: Knowing when to pick your battles is an important skill in surviving your child's adolescent years. This is particularly useful when trying to find alternatives to overreacting with an intense angry response to every act of independence by your Tween.

One extremely helpful first step in generating alternatives is to have a plan beforehand on how you are going to deal with the situations that experience has taught you result in your gut-wrenching physiological anger response. Whenever humanly possible, apply a behavioral consequence for your Tween's action (e.g., grounded for the day) instead of reacting emotionally (screaming). After calming down, then matter-of-factly saying, "You're grounded for two days," and walking away is a lot healthier for you psychologically (i.e., less stress reactions such as headaches and "nervous" stomachs) and better for your relationship with your Tween. It is too easy to do Tween bashing (e.g., "You are no good!") when angry. It is counterproductive to attack your child's self-esteem. Children with low self-esteem are more at risk for rebellious actions that border on self-destruction.

Anger-Arousing Situations	
Problem Situations	Your Thoughts
1.	
2.	
3.	
4.	
5.	
6.	

Alternatives to Anger	
Problems	Alternative Strategies
1.	
2.	
3.	
4.	
5.	
6.	

Develop a list of the problem situations that cause you to lose your temper. Write down these situations and the thoughts that usually accompany the situations.

The first alternative solution to your anger is to *stop* and *think* before you do or say anything—catch yourself and monitor yourself. Say to yourself, "What is it I have to do?" Blowing up will not solve anything. It is, however, guaranteed to make you very, very upset and to immediately trigger a defiant response in turn from your Tween.

Checklists for Tweens

One of the first steps in helping your Tween begin the process of controlling his anger is to complete

Tween Anger Checklist		
Triggers	Tween's Response	Consequences
1.		
2.		
3.		
4.		
5.		

the following table on what triggers his anger (problem definition), what he usually does when his anger is triggered, and what the consequences or outcome of his actions are.

Knowing what provokes anger in your Tween helps you to identify the at-risk situations that are likely in the future to be anger triggers. Being aware of these problematic situations in advance allows you and your child to take preventive actions as soon as the situation arises. As the parent, you will need to have a number of behavioral consequences (e.g., taking away privileges so you can respond as matter-of-factly as humanly possible). For your Tween, he needs to use the *stop* and *think* techniques so he can avoid the behavioral consequence by not overreacting to problematic situations. By having in place a

List of Alternative Behaviors (response)	
Triggers	Positive Alternative Response
1.	
2.	
3.	
4.	
5.	

Tween Thoughts and Feelings		
Anger Triggers	Thoughts	Feelings
1. Mom criticizes the way I clean my room.	"Who cares how I clean my room?"	Sad, frustrated
2.		
3.		
4.		
5.		

behavioral consequence, you motivate your Tween to try to control his temper, since you have now upped the ante.

Another way to further help your preteen learn to manage anger is learning to use breathing exercises when he finds himself in a trigger situation, a good method to diffuse anger. Have him list some of the thoughts he recalls having just before losing control. Have him list his thoughts and feelings in response to specific problem situations.

By having you and your Tween learn some simple relaxation techniques, you are giving each other skills that will help redirect his anger and yours. It is very difficult to be relaxed and angry at the same time. By eliciting a relaxation response, the anger arousal will be diminished to a level that will allow you both to *stop* and *think* first before acting out. The following examples are simple, but highly effective. They can help you both calm down, so you can communicate more rationally when conflict arises. You can't force your Tween to do the exercises. But remind him you are offering him a skill that is certainly a better alternative to being grounded.

Anger Controls

- **Anger button**—Become familiar with those issues that "set you off" and discuss them with the family and your child. Ask that they be aware of and sensitive to your anger buttons and then find out what their anger buttons are. For instance, if your child goes ballistic every time you go in his room and rearrange his CD collection, be aware of this and avoid his territory.
- **Reaction**—Be aware of how you react when you get angry and modify inappropriate responses.
- **Time-out**—Take a time-out for yourself. Go to another room for twenty minutes. Get away from the hot zone.
- **Control-Reinforcement**—Regain control and start over with a positive attitude. Do not hold any grudges.

Battle Stations: Choose Your Battles

One mother was in tears when she simply could not get her point across to her thirteen-year-old daughter. The child refused to listen to what her mother had to say about the way the girl's friend misbehaved at their home. The friend broke an expensive vase and didn't tell anyone, took the girl's necklace and never returned it, and never said "thank you" for the sleepover. Her child refused to acknowledge any of this behavior on her friend's part. She was clearly oppositional to her mother's viewpoint. After much arguing, the mother realized that there was no chance of reaching her daughter. The mom was a chronic complainer about her daughter's friends, and at this point the Tween turned a deaf ear to her.

There is an important lesson to be learned from this mother's conflict. *Choose your battles carefully.* This mom had constant minor complaints about her child's friends, and so when it counted, the daughter didn't listen. The mother lost her ability to impact her daughter's thinking by not being discriminating with her issues. As your Tween gets older and may be involved with kids who are clearly a poor influence, you will need to save the big guns for when it counts. If you let minor infractions go now, your

Tween will know you really mean business when you speak to her about something. Your opinion needs to be listened to and respected. But it is difficult to listen to someone who yells and picks at you constantly.

The Tween years are marked by an increase in parent-adolescent conflicts. These conflicts revolve around your child's striving for more independence at a time when you are torn as to how much freedom you are willing to give. Your child will suddenly argue over curfew, chores, boy-girl interactions, and such issues as pierced ears, hair coloring, baggy pants, short skirts, and spending money. Whether or not these issues escalate into major battles will be determined by how the family reacts. If you lump everything together, you will see your child as a problem, and the issues will become significantly larger. If you deal with each issue individually and problem solve through them, you will be able to handle any child-parent conflict.

Rigid beliefs and expectations will only inflame and illicit angry responses from your child. By saying, "You may never do that," "It's disgusting and so are your friends," you push your child farther away. It is vital to assess your parental rules and demands as your child enters this phase. The line between restriction and overinvolvement is thin.

Parent Support

- Talk to friends who have children the same age.
- Join a school parents' group.
- Buy appropriate parenting psychology books.
- Go to a therapist if you feel too stressed to handle your child.
- Talk to a school counselor or psychologist about age-appropriate behavior.

Negative Interactions

"Don't act so stupid!" yelled one frustrated mom at her obstinate son who refused to listen. Parents are not perfect, and the most loving can be pushed beyond his limits, especially by a nasty-mouthed child with attitude. But if you continually respond negatively, then you run the risk of damaging the relationship with your child.

As your child matures, there will be more and more issues you will disagree on. The way you *both* handle disagreements will determine how a situation will resolve—positively or negatively.

It is not uncommon to be unaware of your negative interactions. On page 61 is a list of typical responses and the preferred positive responses to

| Positive-Negative Response Chart ||
Negative	Positive
Yelling	Talking
Threatening	Offering alternative suggestions
Name-calling	Praising and complimenting
Criticism	Expressing other's point of view
Asking accusative questions	Willingness to listen and ask appropriate questions
Monopolizing the conversation	Allowing the other person to have his say
Demanding	Compromising
Sarcasm	Joking
Acquiescense; overly accepting or agreeing	Expressing your feelings, thoughts, and ideas clearly

your child. This list should be shared with your
Tween so he becomes aware of alternate responses
that he can use when he is angry or frustrated.

~ 6 ~

Discipline

Discipline with a Tween is serious business. This is no longer the world simply of time-outs and "no TV." Discipline can be big guns, especially if your child is grounded and cannot go to an important party—of course, all parties are important at this age. You will receive "the guilts" and a scene out of a soap opera. The dialogue might go something like, "How could you do this to me? I hate you. You are the worst parent. My life is ruined." Holding firm under that kind of verbal pressure from your child might be difficult, but you have to for your sanity and their ultimate good.

As dramatic as this sounds, it isn't. Discipline is where the best parents fall short and do not have good follow-through because it is the most emotionally explosive area of child rearing. Happily, by the time your child is a preteen, you will have a discipline program in place. By this, I mean that your child will know what his boundaries are and what the consequences of inappropriate behavior will be. Even if you do have limits and punishments set, it is best to reiterate basic discipline techniques so that you can add or subtract where you might think it is beneficial. No discipline method is set in stone, and you should be somewhat flexible. For instance, forgetting a homework assignment may warrant a different punishment than lying or getting in a fight at school.

I have never been a spanking advocate. It is especially dangerous to hit Tweens. They're already volatile, and hitting them would only incite them to more anger. You will only feel guilty and distraught. One mother pushed her child and then got pushed back by her thirteen-year-old daughter. The mother was clearly shocked by her child's actions. Spanking a preteen should *never* be an option. There are a number of discipline techniques that will help you establish appropriate punishment for your Tween.

Logical Consequences

Logical consequences are the way to help your Tween take responsibility for his own behavior.

Some parents find it difficult to let their children experience logical consequences because it means letting go of a certain amount of parental control. Like natural consequences, logical consequences are child-based.

Laura learned a tough lesson. She continually refused to cooperate when her volleyball coach gave her direction. She would make silly remarks. She never thought anything would happen to her because she was one of the best players on the team. When Laura pushed too far and talked back to the coach, she was thrown off the team. Laura was shocked. She couldn't believe she was not going to play in the finals. But her coach would not renege. She was off the team! This is a good example of logical consequences. If you *act* like A, then B consequences will follow.

For example, if you do not do your homework or study, then you will most likely not do well on the test. Logical consequences do not always happen at a designated time. Maybe you don't get thrown off the team, or perhaps you pass your test. But usually, if a certain behavior continues, the consequences will catch up to the child, and the impact will be a powerful one.

Logical consequences will help a child to learn to make logical and correct choices. Also, logical consequences will make a Tween accountable for his choices. There will be no one else to blame but himself. A logical consequence violates the rules of cooperation.

There are certain conditions that create logical consequences:

- Logical consequences deal with the present and future—not what happened in the past.
- Logical consequences are based on accountability by the child.
- Logical consequences involve making choices.
- Logical consequences involve mutual respect.

Rules for Using Logical Consequences

- Do not interfere with a consequence. Let your child experience it. For instance, don't talk the coach into letting your child remain on the team.
- Do not talk. Use action.
- Discuss the consequences calmly but firmly.
- Be fair. Use the same consequences for all children.
- Be consistent.
- Do not change the consequence. Stick with your convictions and not what other people feel you should do.

- Do not harp on negative behavior. Once the consequence has been experienced, look for positive behavior.

Natural Consequences

Natural consequences are simply allowing the natural (physical) consequence of a behavior teach the lesson rather than parental nagging, yelling, or threats. Repeated behaviors will not change unless something happens that causes your Tween to *choose* to change. How many times have you asked your child to do something, but he refused? The minute a friend asks, he springs into action. Lessons cannot always be taught. They sometimes have to be learned by doing or not doing something that creates a cause and effect.

For instance, Jamie refused to wear his shin guards to soccer practice. He wouldn't listen to his mom, who warned him that he'd get hurt. Still, he continued to disregard his mother's repeated warnings. Finally, during the practice the week before a finals game, Jamie was kicked in the shin by accident and unable to play in the final game. He was devastated. Although this is a tough lesson to learn, it is one Jamie will never forget.

His mother could have demanded and yelled and punished him for not wearing shin guards, but at some point, the fight to get your Tween to listen is better left to natural consequences. As long as the consequence is not an unsafe or dangerous one, your preteen will "get the point" without your having to say, "I told you so."

The Cut-Eyebrow Story

While sitting at the dinner table, I noticed my daughter's hair hiding half of her face. Her blond locks were falling into her soup. As I brushed her hair aside, I noticed something that took me aback. Her beautiful eyebrows were cut in half. The ends were no longer there.

"What did you do?!" I asked.

She told me she thought her eyebrows were too hairy, and so she and her best friend decided it was time to pluck them. Help! Tweezers were not handy, so she used a razor to shave her perfectly shaped eyebrows. The stubble was already starting to grow back, and I envisioned her new eyebrows as coarse, stubby, and dark.

Yelling at her at this point was useless, since she was clearly miserable with this "plucking-shaving" job. To say she learned her lesson would be putting it mildly. But it was painful to see her so unhappy. Yet, I told her never to touch her eyebrows until she talked to me. Part of my mother-ego was pleased that she had been the recipient of the consequences of her impulsive behavior.

What I was able to do from this mild lesson was to talk about more serious matters. There are consequences you don't want your child to pay, so take advantage of the ones that offer a teaching lesson. Try not to be punitive—no finger shaking, nasty remarks, or "I told you so's." The consequences from your Tween's behavior will be enough. It certainly was in the case of the cut eyebrows.

The Work Chore

There are some minor problems that require a swift and effective discipline technique. When grounding is not the choice, the work chore is a great alternative to a more punitive discipline. The work chore is just that. When your Tween misbehaves, you assign a work chore(s) to him. You can pick a series of chores ahead of time and explain them to your child.

Usually, a work chore will be given for infractions like not listening when you ask your child to do something, talking back, or not doing homework. Give the work chore, and if your child does not comply within five minutes, add an additional work chore. The chores can be assigned for one day or up to a week. Do not sit and discuss or negotiate the work chore. The following are a number of work chore ideas for you to draw from:

Work Chore Ideas

Mow the lawn.
Take out the garbage.
Sweep the floor.
Empty the dishwasher.
Clean the toilets.
Wash the car.
Sweep out the garage.
Clean the fireplace.
Rake leaves.
Feed and take out the dog.
Clean the stove.
Clean your closet and drawers.
Wash and fold laundry.

Removal of Privileges

Removing privileges means taking away something from your child for a specified period of time. This could mean a material object—such as the telephone or CD player—or a nonmaterial object like watching television or using the Internet. This discipline technique hits home. Kids detest having anything taken away from them.

When Carole had her phone privileges taken away for one day for talking back to her mom, she was miserable. It is important to take away a privilege that will have an impact on your Tween. Make sure you don't take something away for too long a period of time.

Grounding

Grounding is a more serious method of discipline that may be used to teach your child the consequences of breaking rules (inappropriate behavior).

Grounding means

- Staying in her own room unless eating meals, working on chores, or attending school
- Performing required chores
- Following house rules
- No television
- No telephone calls
- No stereo, radio, etc.
- No video games or other games or toys
- No bike riding

- No friends over or going to friends' houses
- No outside social activities (e.g., movies, going out to dinner, etc.)

Being grounded does *not* mean

- Nagging
- Reminding about jobs to be done
- Discussing the grounding
- Explaining the rules

If the grounding seems to be lasting an excessively long time, check to be sure that your child's life is dull enough during the grounding. Make sure you are not providing a lot of attention in the form of nagging. Grounding is effective when your child follows the rules more often and is aware of the consequences of breaking them. Be sure you have a babysitter available on short notice in case your child is grounded and unable to accompany you on a planned family outing.

The battles during these years are plentiful. However, armed with good behavioral tools, information, and a sense of humor—and lots of love and positive reinforcement—you will get through them.

~ 7 ~

I'll Talk, and Then You Talk

Communication is the key component to establishing a good relationship with your Tween. It's what most parents interviewed complained about the most. The Tween years are difficult because you go from total adoration by your sweet child to a Tween who barely speaks to you. This is a shock that comes on fast and leaves parents reeling. That is why good communication will keep the door open during these difficult years and the even more trying years of teenage adolescence.

The Thin Line

There is a line that will soon be drawn by your child—your preteen. It is a thin line between involvement and disassociation. You will have trouble with this line at first because it is invisible and easy to cross. It will happen quickly, usually without your noticing. One day you will ask your Tween about her friends and what's going on socially, and she will shut you out. Her door will be closed, and a big sign will go up saying, "Keep Out, Knock First, DO NOT ENTER."

Your first instinct might be to

- tear down the signs
- tear out your hair
- tear at your heart

But before you get too hysterical, try to be reasonable. None of these will accomplish very much in trying to find a balance with your child. Tearing down the signs (literally and figuratively) will only serve to further alienate your child.

Getting attention from your Tween is like begging to be noticed while standing behind a brick wall. Your Tween is seeking independence now, and you are standing in his way of trying to mature, especially when asking for hugs and kisses. This will be a very difficult time for parents because it is not easy to give up your "baby"—the child that you nurtured and cuddled. Not that some children aren't still affectionate, but most at this age do not want an overly demonstrative parent. It is embarrassing and uncool to be cuddling and kissing Mom and Dad in public. Maybe if you beg, you can get a hug in private.

What is important is that you continually tell your child how much he is loved and valued. Don't stop trying to sneak those hugs and kisses because secretly he wants your attention and love. The crazy ups and downs of preteen life are experiences that you will have to roll with.

Many parents go into a depression as their children start to get older. Somehow parents start to feel they are aging, and they may feel as if they are not needed as much. But this is not true. In fact, your child needs you more now than ever before. Your encouragement, guidance, and love are his anchors in what will become a very rocky sea. Do not discount your importance.

Dr. Laurence Steinberg cites in his book, *Crossing Paths: How Your Child's Adolescence Triggers Your Own Crisis*, that parents who did well during the tumultuous preteen years had three common threads to successful parenting during this time:

• They had interests outside of being parents and made sure they indulged them.

- They had a positive attitude and remained connected and loving to their adolescent children and did not expect that adolescence was going to be a "nightmare."
- They regularly discussed their feelings with friends, spouses, and/or therapists.

It is important to note that there is nothing wrong with your feelings as long as they are just that—feelings. Parents should never act out jealously or in anger. When your child starts to pull away, you may even feel depressed and lonely. Couples often think about having another child to fill that void. But you can keep the lines open and loving with your Tween if you work at it. You can stay a part of his life and not feel pushed aside.

Good communication with your Tween will take you well beyond those years and into the teen years when communication skills are vital. Working on a positive way to keep the doors open to a good relationship with your Tween can avert a family breakdown.

Listening

Taking time to *really listen*, understand, and being open and honest with your preteen makes her feel cared about and valued. Developing skills to listen to your child's feelings is important. These skills will help you with your child's problem and your own. Do you ever wonder why your child doesn't listen after you've told him the same thing a hundred times? Your Tween has heard you, but chosen not to listen. How many times do you criticize, threaten, question, pity, judge, or reassure your child when he is angry or upset? Does your child get even more upset by your response?

Most people who are upset usually merely want someone to listen to their feelings. When parents immediately start giving advice or asking questions or judging a situation, they do not give their children a chance to be heard. They deny the child's feelings, and in turn their Tween may ignore, rebel, or become discouraged. The attitude is "Why bother?"

Good communication starts with a respect for someone's feelings and opinions. But first it should be determined whose problem it is. Sometimes we intervene in problems that our preteens should own and work out. We can become parental enablers if we are constantly bailing our child out of a problem rather than guiding him through the steps to solve it himself.

Owning a problem refers to determining who is responsible for handling a situation. For instance, if a child is having difficulty with a peer, he owns the problem. Too often parents get involved in the social lives of their kids, settling arguments, conflicts, and disputes only to have disastrous results. You should only intervene in a child's problem if the child's safety is involved.

By taking over a child's problems you teach him to be dependent. Your goal should be to create an independent child. Therefore, you need to determine the following: Who does the problem really affect? and Who is responsible for the problem?

You own problems that involve your responsibility as a parent. When Johnny is skateboarding at full speed down the hill without a helmet, it is clear that you own the problem. You are responsible for his health and safety.

When Josh told his dad, Alan, he no longer wanted to play soccer, Alan was furious. He felt that Josh should play soccer. All the boys did. Alan had. But it was Josh's right to decide that he didn't want to play soccer. The problem is Alan's—not Josh's. Alan needs to come to terms with why he feels so compelled to push his son into playing or allow Josh to follow his own interests.

The better way to avoid parent-child conflict is by putting the problem responsibility where it belongs. As a parent you can choose a number of ways to have your child solve a problem, depending on how receptive and cooperative your Tween is.

Problem Choices

- Listen only and offer no solution.
- Listen and offer problem-solving solutions.
- Rely on natural and logical consequences—letting any negative consequences of your child's actions result in a learning experience.

Problem Solving and Decision Making

"My life is over!" exclaimed one twelve-year-old who was faced with going to "the party of the year" at her school or the party of her close friend who attended another school. The parties were on the same day and almost at the same time. Her school friends pressed her to go to their party, and her good buddy said she'd be hurt if she didn't come to hers. The girl felt she had not only a big problem, but no choices whatsoever. In other words, she felt like she was boxed in.

Many Tweens are so emotionally charged that they see no alternatives to problems because they have poor coping and problem-solving skills. These stressors can lead to serious problems. Therefore, it is vital that you help your Tween through problem-solving and decision-making steps.

Through problem solving, many conflicts can be resolved with friends, family, and teachers. Problem solving empowers people. Their anxiety levels are reduced because they see alternatives and eventually make a decision.

Melanie did not have the proper behavioral tools to encourage Megan and help her focus on her positive traits. Megan's internal evaluation of herself was negative. She felt awkward and ugly. Melanie only validated this by trying to fix what was wrong with Megan. Megan needed words of support and acceptance from her mother. If Megan did want to make changes then she needed the proper problem-solving tools to access changes realistically.

The hysteria of the Tween years can be averted by some simple strategies. Perhaps the best way to help your Tween is to teach him how to cope by problem solving. Your Tween will avoid the pitfalls of rash, hysterical behavior or waiting until the problem is so bad, the alternatives are few. By assessing a situation and then making informed choices, you will be teaching patience, tolerance, and maturity.

The following problem-solving techniques will

Problems to Be Solved with Your Tween

Problem 1:

Problem 2:

Problem 3:

Problem 4:

Problem 5:

Parent-Adolescent Problem Chart

What is the specific conflict situation?_____

_____

Where does the conflict occur?_____

_____

When does the conflict occur?_____

_____

Who else is involved as part of the conflict?_____

_____

Why does the conflict occur?_____

_____

How do you respond and feel when the conflict occurs?_____

_____

_____

Parent-Adolescent Solutions Chart	
Alternative Solutions: _____	

	Parent–Generated	Tween–Generated
Solution 1 _____		
Solution 2 _____		
Solution 3 _____		
Solution 4 _____		
Solution 5 _____		

help both you and your child solve problems that sometimes seem (especially to a Tween) unsolvable. Coping and problem-solving skills will be useful throughout your child's life.

Problem-Solving Techniques

- **Define** the problem. Try to be as specific as possible.
- **Search** for ways to solve the problem. Write down a number of ways that you might be able to solve the problem.
- **Choose** your idea. Pick the way to solve your problem that seems the best.
- **Evaluate** the effectiveness of your plan and rework it if it didn't work.

The following charts can help your Tween get in touch with his feelings. They can also be an invaluable guide for parents who may not really be aware of their teenagers' inner thoughts. Tweens are not always open with parents. They think parents (all adults) don't understand them. Thus, they hold a lot of their fears and thoughts inside.

Give the charts to your Tween. Have him check off the boxes that apply to him. Then ask if he would be willing to share them with you. Do not

Behavior Checklist

School

I avoid tests. _____
I don't like to study. _____
I'm not spending enough time studying. _____
I can't keep my mind on my studies. _____
I move around too much in class. _____
I have trouble with homework. _____
I don't like school. _____
Reading is a problem for me. _____
Writing is difficult for me. _____
I avoid oral reports. _____
Other _____

Family

I don't like having to ask parents for money. _____
I want more freedom at home. _____
I fight with sisters. _____
I fight with brothers. _____
Other _____

Friends

I get too little change to go to parties. _____
I don't have enough time for play and fun. _____
I have trouble making friends. _____
I have trouble keeping friends. _____
I am too easily led by other people. _____
I pick the wrong kinds of friends. _____
I don't have as much fun as other kids. _____
I have no place to go to be with friends. _____
I get nervous when I'm with girls. _____
I get nervous when I'm with boys. _____
I have trouble keeping a conversation going. _____
I don't know what to do on a date. _____
I get into fights. _____
Learning how to dance is hard for me. _____
I have trouble dressing nicely. _____

Imagery Worksheet

Underline the words that you agree with:

I picture school as:

Happy, hard, fun, lots of work, boring, easy, trouble, something to escape, full of friends, a lonely place, warm, strict, prison, a place to get high, nothing but trouble

Other: _____

I picture my family as:

Crazy, loving, doing things together, never talking, always angry, a good place to be, better than many others, awful, a loving place, a place to avoid

Other: _____

I picture my friends as:

Trustworthy, loyal, selfish, two-faced, shallow, always present, accepting, deceitful, troublemakers, friendly, in a clique

Other: _____

I picture myself as:

Wanting to run away from home, clumsy, awkward, good looking, smart, a daydreamer, not smart enough, not good looking, too tall, too short, fooling everybody

Other: _____

judge them. Do not take them as a personal affront. Feelings are changeable—and volatile for kids. Just letting them get them out and share them is a positive step forward.

When you feel totally stifled by your efforts to solve your problems, try the following "pats on the back," which help put your acute problems in perspective:

1. Stop and think.
2. Take a deep breath and calm down.
3. Say, "I can handle this."
4. What is the problem?
5. What are some solutions?
6. What's my first choice?
7. OK, let's try it out.
8. How am I doing?
9. Is this OK, or do I need to try my next choice?
10. All right, this is going OK.
11. Nice job! You handled this.

If the desired outcome is not achieved after troubleshooting through all the problem-solving steps, then determine whether you need additional information or assistance from a knowledgeable source such as a friend or professional. When a problem situation appears unsolvable, then attempt to determine which components of the situation may in fact be solvable.

Body Talk

One mother confessed to a friend, "My son, Tony, talked and talked today, but didn't say a word." This mother was not "talking" about words but *body language*. Her son, with his crossed arms, fidgeting legs, and lack of eye contact, had given this mom a clue that something was up. She pressed him gently by asking, "Is something bothering you?" At first Tony denied there was anything wrong. But when his body talk clearly said something different from his verbal cues, she kept asking. Eventually, Tony revealed that he got in trouble in school and had to go to the principal's office, and he was given a last warning.

Body talk will tell you a lot about your child. Watch his body, his eyes, and listen to his voice. If your child says, "Everything is fine," you might want to point out that his body talk says something else. This observation will usually open the door for your Tween to talk about his feelings.

Body talk applies to parents as well. If your body is tightly closed and your voice is hostile, your Tween will most likely not listen to your words no matter how friendly they are. Nonverbal communication is often more potent than verbal communication.

Feelings Count

Parents can get so caught up in their work and responsibilities as a spouse, friend, parent, helper, and worker that they forget to take time to stop and listen to their preteen's feelings. Many parents are defensive or overly worried every time their Tween is upset or angry and responds inappropriately. Because of the emotional nature of most Tweens, it is probably best to arm yourself with some good listening-feeling skills. These skills will be positive for you and your child, and ultimately can make the relationship better between parent and child.

The key is to pick up on the message your Tween is sending you. Tween messages are often like Morse Code or a complete new foreign language that you will have to learn. But it is better to speak your child's language than to be in the dark!

Tweens don't want constant scolding or advice. It is a quick way to have her tune out. The *way* we listen is important. For instance, Missy comes home and says, "I got a lousy grade in an open-book test today because I left my book at home." Your usual response might be, "Well, that wasn't smart," or "You better be more responsible."

You will be able to get your point across to your child if you embrace her feelings by saying, "You must have really been upset today." You are acknowledging that you understand. Try to avoid lecturing, judgments, and criticism. Once you reflect what your child seems to be feeling, she will be apt to open up more often. Also, don't demand that your child share his feelings. Respect his personal space. You can get further with your Tween if you let him know that his behavior affects you. Do not say, "I can't stand you." Instead use words like, "I don't like it when you act this way. It makes me feel disrespected."

If by now you are thinking, "What about me?" the answer is simple. You can express your feelings to your child in the same manner that you reflect his. But don't fall into the blame trap. Your Tween is not responsible for your feelings—you are.

Hostile Feelings

Whatever you do, don't let angry feelings build up. Encourage your child to discuss any angry feelings toward you at appropriate times (family meetings) and in appropriate ways. It is easy to lash out at your Tween. After an exhausting day, you might want to be greeted with a hug and a smile. Instead, you get a moody, untalkative preteen. It is important to let your child know how you feel before you let the message turn angry. An angry message can become hostile in tone. Your Tween will most likely become defensive and hostile back. This will create negative interaction that will go nowhere.

Often, your angry feelings are about you and not your child. Your internal anger, disappointment, and fears play into your child's behavior, and kick off your angry feelings. If there is constant anger and yelling in a relationship, then the communication between parent and child needs to be looked at.

There are some effective ways to open positive communication lines with your Tween. Hopefully, the following will be helpful:

- Open up conversation—Ask your child to share his feelings by asking interested, concerned, but not charged, questions.
- Do not force conversation—If your child does not want to share, don't force the issue. Allow him his privacy.
- Share your feelings—Let your child know what bothers you and what hurts you.

- Do not interrogate your child—Tweens can't stand it when parents ask a million probing questions.
- Don't overanalyze everything your child says.

Opening the door to talk will help you get through these sometimes trying years. Once you open that door, keep it open because you will need to have an open dialogue once your child hits his serious teenage years.

There are no hard and fast rules about communicating with your Tween, but the lines can quickly break down at this age. Your child will selectively tune you out, and it may be difficult to get your point across when you are talking to a blank wall.

Here are some suggestions on how to break through the barrier that may be keeping you from effectively communicating with your Tween. Use all or a combination of techniques:

- Never give up.
- Don't let your child tune you out.
- Always engage him in conversation.
- Ask questions.
- Show interest in his life, friends, and school.

Perhaps the best way to communicate now is to talk and keep talking. By that I mean let your child know that you are:

- Always available to talk
- Ready to listen to anything he wants to tell you without judgment
- Eager to help him work out the problem no matter what it is, even if he did something wrong
- Always able to make time for your child with family meetings

Family Meetings

The family meeting is one of the ways you can keep "talking with your adolescent." The meetings should give each member of the family a chance to vent feelings and take part in family decisions. Preteens want to share their feelings but often feel uncomfortable about revealing their thoughts about more complex issues like the opposite sex, drugs, friends, school-related issues, and the world at large.

Rules for Family Meetings

- A family meeting occurs at a specific time and place, usually weekly, but some families have meetings more often or less often.
- The meeting is a place where decisions are made, feelings are vented, and opinions are given.

- Each member of the family talks without interruption, for a specified period of time (usually about five minutes).
- You can ask for ideas on how to solve a problem, but don't impose your ideas unless asked for by a member of the family.
- Respect the family's privacy, and don't take issues out of the meeting.
- Give positive feedback and encouragement.

How to Talk to a Tween

One mother confessed that she was always tense around her Tween. "Every time I try to talk to her, she snaps back. Then I yell. Then she yells, and we argue. We disagree on everything—or rather—she disagrees with everything I say! I feel like I'm getting nowhere fast!"

This typical scenario is Tween talk at its best—or worst! Tweens are not easy to communicate with. They are pulling away, and just your presence represents (figuratively) rules, authority, and lack of independence. But in reality, your Tween wants your input and approval. In fact, she needs it more now than ever. She just doesn't know it. There are ways to engage your Tween in meaningful conversation with an argument. You have to be a bit more clever (remember the toddler years) and be respectful of her space.

According to several family therapists, preteens want to be included in discussions about family matters such as vacation choices, the purchase of a pet, and so on. They would also like to be privy to more serious subjects that you discuss (e.g., sex, drugs, and money matters).

Without being abrasive, start opening up to your Tween about your feelings about certain subjects. Be open and candid, but mindful that your child is still learning about the world at large and may be impressionable. For instance, you might want to discuss current events in the news and then talk about your feelings and your child's on a particular news story. This way, you can give your own opinions and discuss the pros and cons of an issue and explain any aspects that your child may not grasp.

Don't talk "down" to your child—Don't act like he is too young or immature to understand topics such as religion, politics, war, or homosexuality. A 13-year-old has been exposed to all of this information through MTV, the Internet, and movies. It is better to be open and discuss touchy subjects rather than pretend they don't exist.

Don't get too personal—Preteens do not want to tell you about their personal lives. Stay away! But they do want to discuss *your* personal life. They want to know all about what it was like when you were their age. They love to look at old pictures. They want to know what you wore, what music you listened to, what you looked like, and what your life was like in the "old days." These threads of information give your child a sense of continuity to his life, and this is important. Continuity helps him see where his life has been and where it is going. You are the anchor for this thread. Feel free to talk about your life. This will open up a discussion about your child's life, and eventually he will talk about his plans and thoughts for his life and future.

Don't give attitude—If you haven't already noticed, young adolescents can give off major attitude. Often, attitude is a reflection of the person you are speaking to. For instance, seeing your young child mature and become a preteen can cause conflicting internal feelings in you. You might be upset by the loss of your little boy or girl. So you internalize your feelings and become frustrated. When your preteen speaks to you like a more mature person, you may react to him as if he is being disrespectful or abusive, when in effect, he is responding as a preteen would. So what you might see as attitude is merely a reflection of your attitude. You can change this negative interplay by:

- Being more positive—use positive reinforcement with your child.
- Smiling at your child a lot.
- Using humor rather than being reactive to what he says.
- Discussing your feelings with your child and spouse regularly.

What Not to Say to a Tween

Beware the Tween twin. She will emulate your behavior, listen to adult conversations, and parrot back information at the wrong time. This especially hit home when Gerry's son Brad started asking his grandmother personal questions about what she was leaving him in her will. Gerry almost fell on the floor but then remembered a conversation he had with his wife about personal items his mother wanted him to have when she died.

Tweens listen to adult conversations and don't know what to censor. They think they are mature and can handle what they are hearing, but this is often not the case. A preteen should not be present during serious adult conversation. Tweens may misinterpret what they've heard, discuss your conversation with the wrong person, or be worried and frightened by your words for no reason.

If you are in an argument and your child is present, you may say things to your spouse or partner that you are sorry for later but leave a lasting impact on your Tween. Preteens are like sponges. They will also imitate your actions. The way you treat waiters, workers, salespeople—anyone—will affect how they treat these people. Respect is displayed, not just spoken about.

Values

Evan told his teacher to "take a hike." His parents were shocked. They couldn't believe that their sweet little boy Evan could talk like that. But Evan was no longer a little boy. He was a Tween. Tweens test their boundaries more and are less willing to deal with punishment because they have less fear. Almost every Tween will at sometime or another engage in negative behavior—behavior that may be aggressive, dishonest, disrespectful, or antisocial. It is the degree and consistency of these behaviors that signal real trouble. It is more difficult with Tweens who can get peer reward for antisocial behavior.

That is why it is vital that adults follow rules, explain rules to their children, and discuss the consequences of breaking rules. A parent should let his Tween know how rules in society work and help him to understand the impact of his actions on himself and those around him.

Parents who are overly harsh create a child who is preoccupied with punishment. The Tween obeys rules only to avoid punishment, not because he understands that he should do the right thing. If a child is spending his time doing what is right to avoid being caught, he doesn't understand that honesty and fairness are moral decisions that form the basis of one's character and how he acts the rest of his life.

Parents must model good values for their children to follow. If you lie, cheat, and steal in business, how can you expect your child to act differently? Money oftentimes becomes too coveted by parents who teach their children to value currency above all else. When adults are observant and fair, children will usually learn to follow society's rules and understand their limits and boundaries.

Much of this book touches on the subject of *values*. The way you model behavior, discipline your preteen, handle problems, and communicate will set the tone for the values you establish in your family. Values go to the root of who you and your family are—how you treat other people, your moral fiber, and what priorities you have established. It is probably just as important to live with and model good values for your child as it is to talk about values.

Because Tweens are becoming more independent thinkers, you will want to explore the subject of values rather than impose them. You can't demand your child act a certain way, but you can use hypothetical situations. For example, try to put your child in another person's shoes. Ask questions. "How would you feel if someone hurt your feelings like that?" "Do you think it's OK to take something from a store?" "What if it were your store, and you worked for years to buy the merchandise?" Trying to create empathy for others helps a young person to be more sensitive. Be giving and charitable so your child will follow by example.

Values are often based on having one's priorities in order. Fill out the parent priority list (page 102). It will give you a clearer picture of what your individual priorities are and help your Tween establish his own priorities.

There are some things that form your child's personality that are in your control, like values and self-esteem. Then there are other things like heredity and peer influence that are out of your control. As much as possible, you need to explore values with your Tween. This is a fine line, since parents tend to impose their values on their children. They threaten that if their children don't obey, they will be severely punished. This is punitive and usually will push your child away from you. Rather, it is best to use good role modeling. Tweens are quick to point out to their parents, "You do it, so why can't I?"

Tweens want answers for everything. Perhaps the greatest gift you can give to your child is teaching him how to cope with problems, anger, and how to treat other people. These life skills can carry him far in life. But you must show, not just tell, him. How you react to life's difficult situations, solve family problems, treat people, and communicate will be the model for him to follow.

Tween Years Parent Checklist

- Set an example by your own behavior.
- Pick your battles. Don't let the small things add up.
- Stay calm while the storm rages.
- Don't use comparisons.
- Try not to "give" guilt.
- Use the problem-solving method often.

Parent Priority List
Write your priorities from 1 to 10.
1.
2.
3.
4.
5.
6.
7.
8.
9.
10.

Tween Priority List
Write your priorities from 1 to 10.
1.
2.
3.
4.
5.
6.
7.
8.
9.
10.

~ 8 ~

Home Rules

Home rules will help you keep—or not keep—your sanity. They are the basic training tools of living with a Tween. If your rules aren't firmly established, then you've left the door open for problems. Know what you're dealing with, and you'll be more connected with your child and the world he lives in.

Rock What?

Music is very important to Tweens. For some it's the focus of their existence and the bane of yours. You may find all of your child's allowance going to buy CDs and tapes. You may also hate the music your child chooses, and most of the time it is best to get ear plugs or close the door. Trying to change their taste in music is useless. I can actually remember my own mother thinking the Beatles would be the downfall of our generation. Yet, their music seems so benign in light of today's gangster rap and underground music.

Music is the memory landmark of youth and an important part of your child's life. His choices are usually based on who's new, young, hip, and experimental. This is OK. Try to really listen to the music. Hear it like your child is hearing it. Talk to him about the music, and don't be negative.

The Telephone

You will never view the telephone the same way again once your Tween gets hold of it. Tweens treat telephones like physical extensions of themselves. The phone conversations range from frivolous to active, inactive, and serious.

The *frivolous* call is usually to a good friend, and there is a lot of giggling, strange sounds, and inane conversation taking place for hours on end. The *active* call revolves around sports, school friends, and basically is dialed in the hopes of getting much needed information. There is dialogue that gets passed back and forth from one friend to another. After many phone calls, a decision is made. The *inactive* call involves two friends doing homework together. There is very little talk time—much breathing—and an occasional, "What's your answer?" These nonconversations can monopolize your telephone for hours.

Then, there is the *serious* call. This is usually talk about boy/girl troubles and is discussed behind closed doors. Good luck trying to get your child off the phone when it's serious. At least a dozen phone calls back and forth to solve the problem or spread the gossip can occur. If you infer these calls are unnecessary, you will get a dirty look. Do not underestimate the "serious" conversation. What if these calls, especially the serious conversations, come the night before your child has a big test or right before dinner at grandma's? You now have a dilemma.

This is why phone rules are important. Otherwise, you may have a telephone Tween gone rampant.

Telephone Rules

- No talking before homework and chores are completed.
- Limit talk time to 30 minutes total on school nights, one hour (at a time) on the weekend.
- No phone calls after 9 P.M.

- Tell your child to ask friends not to call continuously throughout the night and not before or past the agreed-upon hours.
- No talking during mealtimes.
- If your child misbehaves or breaks the rules, take away phone privileges.

Computer Chit Chat

America Online (AOL) is like a chant in our house. I refused to go on-line until my child tortured me into it. "AOL, AOL, AOL, AOL." I heard these words ringing in my head day and night. Whatever on-line services you may end up choosing, be aware. Don't just sign on and then sign off. The Internet can be a scary place to navigate. From adult chat rooms to sexually explicit junk mail, it is your parental responsibility to monitor your Tween's computer on-line interaction.

There are ways to block certain chat rooms by requesting Child or Teen Service. But, and this is a big one, a savvy computer hacker can get in wherever he wants. My advice is to glance over your Tween's shoulder and see exactly who he or she is communicating with. Internet browsers retain "history" files that you can view, which include listings of pages visited. Set up strict rules regarding on-line chat and pull the plug if your child is getting into areas that are clearly inappropriate.

TV Time

Television watching needs to be monitored if you are going to have a child who reads and does homework without staring at the tube continuously. Some parents forbid TV watching. Others are couch potatoes themselves. Try to find a medium position. Follow some simple rules:

- Keep the television turned off during meals. This way, you can have an active family conversation.
- Be aware of your own television watching. Choose to read or listen to music more often.
- Only allow TV times, certain hours, and special programs. That way, television is a reward.
- De-emphasize television by emphasizing other activities: sports, family games, reading, music, and art projects.

Just Get Dressed

When Sue's twelve-year-old daughter Amy changed her outfit seven times, Sue knew she was in for big trouble. The child stomped out of her room in tears. "I have nothing to wear to Erin's party!"

Of course, Sue made the mistake of trying to advise her daughter, telling her what was inappropriate and what looked good. Amy argued with her mom about every choice until the two of them were at each others' throats. A major clothes war ensued. Clothing becomes very important to Tweens. Clothes define who they are and set Tweens apart socially. It symbolizes their independence.

Debbie refused to go out with her eleven-year-old daughter until Ashley changed her clothes. Debbie felt Ashley's colorful, "hip," somewhat way-out outfit was ugly. Another all-out war over clothes was happening. But the clothes issue went on for years. Debbie had conservative taste and refused to understand her daughter's way-out taste in clothes.

If you don't want to spend the next five or six years arguing about clothes, then try to find a reasonable approach to this dilemma. Remember clothes are a way for your Tween to express individuality. As long as your child is not dressed too suggestively or inappropriately for the weather or a specific activity, it is best to let it go.

Your child is not an extension of you—not a doll to be dressed up according to who you are. Let your child have this form of normal teenage expression.

If no body parts are showing, there are no major rips or holes, then take a deep breath and enjoy the time with your Tween. I guarantee that in a few years she will start looking like you right down to your shoes.

The Mess

Tweens are notorious slobs. If your Tween's room is a mess, he is normal. Girls especially like to try on dozens of outfits and let their clothes fall where they may. It is not unusual to find rotting fruit and year-old candy crusted in a drawer or behind a bed somewhere. Tweens have no concept of order and seem to focus on the end result. They are not bothered by clutter and mess. Usually, a parent will clean up after her Tween, but when the sloppy pattern gets out-of-hand, something has to be done.

There are two ways to approach the problem. You can let your child wallow in her mess or start taking privileges away if her room is not cleaned up. Aim for a happy medium. Before you allow your child to go out with friends, his bed must be made, his clothes picked up, and all papers and trash put in the garbage can. This is not asking too much. But don't expect a dust-free, neat-as-a-pin room. It is not the nature of the beast. If all else fails, let your

Tween live in his mess until he can't stand it any longer. Just close his door and only venture in at risk to your health and sanity.

Bedtime

When I wrote books for parents of toddlers, I talked about dressing and bedtime difficulties with little ones. Although this might seem strange, you can avoid major fights by establishing and talking about nighttime curfews and bedtimes. Your child is not too old to set down these rules. Although you might have to be more flexible, it is important to communicate the "bottom line."

For instance, if your child says he has to stay up until midnight in order to finish a project, this should not be allowed. The project should have been started and time-managed earlier—last-minute slap-dash hysteria and exhaustion are not the answer. On the other hand, if your child's normal bedtime on school nights is 9 P.M., you might let him stay up for an extra hour or so to put last-minute touches on the project. Most Tweens are not ready for bed at 9 P.M., and many do well on less sleep than when they were younger. Most eleven- to thirteen-year-olds I interviewed went to sleep at 10 P.M. They settled in their rooms at 9 P.M. but didn't actually fall asleep until later. On the weekend, most Tweens get to bed around 11:30 P.M. or midnight.

Privacy

Privacy is a huge issue with preteens. This is a time when not only will you not get the information you seek verbally, but you better not go searching for it anywhere in your child's room. Diaries, journals, and letters become sacred domain, and if you invade this area of your Tween's, you may lose his trust for years to come.

It is difficult to let go of the controls with a Tween. The only time you would ever consider looking through your child's personal belongings is if you seriously considered that your child might be involved with drugs or illegal activity that might lead to worse consequences. Do not use this excuse to go digging when you know in your heart that your child is not involved in this type of activity. Preteens need their space and sense of privacy. They are establishing a new autonomy, just as they did when they were toddlers. You let your young child feel a bit of power and independence, and now you have to let your older child have the same sense of freedom.

The decisions that you will have to make regarding your child will not be easy. What you ask, how you ask it, and when you ask will determine how much your child tells you. If you continually grill her, she will turn a deaf ear. It is often best to let your child come to you. Let her know that you are willing to listen without judgment anytime, but don't be surprised if you don't get the information you would like.

Use other parents to be your partners. Often your child will discuss private issues with their friends' parents. Have a pact that you will be willing to share important information about each other's child, but that you cannot go back and question or attack. This is part of the parenting bond that is so necessary as your child becomes an adolescent.

Money and Allowance

If you can accomplish the vitally important task of teaching your child not only the value of money but how to handle money and finances, then you should be congratulated. Money issues cause some of the more profound problems for individuals and result in major rifts in relationships. Children are required to go to school and learn a variety of subjects, but there are no courses on how to balance a checkbook, save for the future, invest their funds, or use their knowledge to make money.

By the time a child is ten, he should get an allowance, have his own savings account, be required to pay for certain unnecessary extras, distribute a small portion of his money to a worthy cause, and know the price of things. It is ironic that money, as powerful as it is, is not discussed with children. Most parents think it is improper to talk about money with a child. But then when their son or daughter spends or asks for things that are frivolous and seems to have a general disregard for what things cost, the parents get angry. How many times have you heard the saying "Money doesn't grow on trees"? It has almost become a cliché.

A Money Plan

Every family needs a money plan; that is, a plan on how money is to be treated and dealt with in the family. Not every money plan will be the same because every family handles money differently. But there are some guidelines for teaching your Tween sound money values.

Allowance and Savings

The old-fashioned piggy bank is the first lesson in saving money. It is probably best to initially establish goals. Johnny wanted to buy a bicycle. So his dad helped him set a time frame and an amount that he needed to save. Johnny started saving his pennies and the loose change his parents gave him. He saved money that he earned doing extra chores around the house. He wanted to have a bike in six months. His dad offered to pay $50 toward the $102 bike. Johnny did save the money and bought his bike in five months. He was extremely proud of his participation in the purchase of his bicycle. He felt a sense of pride and accomplishment. Most importantly, he learned that money has value.

There are different schools of thought about giving an allowance. Some parents feel an allowance should be given without chores attached. Others feel strongly that an allowance is given for work done—like a job. Striking a balance between the two is probably the best approach. But you must make the decision as to whether you want to hold back an allowance if the chores are not completed. For a child who is seriously saving for something that he wants, not getting that allowance can have a big impact.

Allowance Chart

- Set a reasonable amount of money as an allowance. The going rate seems to be between $3 and $6 a week, depending on the age of the child.

- Let your child know what he might be expected to pay for with his allowance. For instance, his money pays for "junkie junk"—posters, face glitter, trinkets, baseball cards, CDs, and tapes.
- You will withhold their allowance for the following: refusing to do chores without a valid excuse (such as studying for a test, drama production, or soccer playoffs). Otherwise, their allowance should become theirs.

You should encourage, guide, and provide all of the necessary information on saving and spending money. Demanding that they spend their allowance on what you deem important is counter-productive.

Also, remember how *you* handle your money is probably the biggest lesson you can teach your Tween. If you are frivolous, do not give to charity, and always have money problems, there is a good possibility that your child will model your actions.

Chores

When I hear the word "chores," I am reminded of kids from years past who lived on a farm and got up at 5 A.M. to milk the cows, feed the pigs, and clean out the barn before going to school. Today's children are far less chore-oriented but rather leisure-oriented. Tweens think chores are taking a bath and doing their homework. Setting the table, taking out the trash, and "cleaning" their rooms are considered burdens—not chores. The moans and groans that accompany these tasks attest to their veracity.

Kids are so overprogrammed with afterschool activities, music, dance, computer, art, and athletics that by the time they sit down to eat and do their homework, it is time to go to bed. Their lives are filled up from morning until night. As a result, parents are not as aggressive in demanding that chores be done. Of course, helping with the family is crucial to teaching a sense of responsibility. Everyone in the family should have some participation in the daily routines, but the degree of participation may need to be curtailed.

Successful and timely completion of homework should be considered an expected responsibility. It is not too much to ask children to set and clear the table, make their beds, pick up their clothes, and take out the trash. Many two-working parent families need their Tween to take on added chores, and your child should be willing to be part of the family.

One mother was so frustrated with her Tween's sloppiness that she gave up. She informed her child that if she wouldn't clean up her room neither would anyone else. Her daughter could live in filth until she cleaned it up. The child laughed, but not for long. When the clothes were piled so high she couldn't find a thing clean to wear and bugs started to invade her room, the girl begged for a bottle of Mr. Clean and a sponge.

This is a good illustration of logical consequences. Sometimes the yelling and cajoling are simply not worth the fight. When you back off and let the consequences of your Tween's own choices and behavior take over, you may be surprised to see a big turnaround. The best part is that the decision to improve will come from your child, not as a result of your threats.

To Sit or Not to Sit?

It is easy to be paranoid in today's world of violence and crime. People used to view their neighbors as extended family but now often wonder if they can be trusted. At twelve, most kids used to be babysitting other children. Today, it is questionable whether or not your Tween needs her own baby-sitter. This is a personal and difficult call to make because the decision is based on many factors.

What Determines If You Need a Baby-Sitter?

- Where you live
- The maturity of your child
- Your home security
- The duration and distance of your time away
- The age of your Tween
- The number and ages of other children in the house
- How responsible your child is
- If there is an adult nearby

Many children are fearful of staying home alone. Others don't mind being alone, but are not responsible enough to take care of another, younger sibling. The "better safe than sorry" way is the best approach in deciding if you should hire a baby-sitter. For a child under eleven, it is best to have an older person in the home when you leave.

For twelve- and thirteen-year-olds who don't want a sitter, do a test run. Go out for no more than an hour or two during the day. Assess how your child does when you're gone. If he is OK, then try an hour one evening. Four or five hours should be your limit when going out and leaving your Tween at home.

Staying Alone Rules

- Set up a list of rules.
- Go over the rules with your child.
- Post important emergency numbers by the phone.
- Check in with your child once or twice during the evening.
- Make sure your Tween knows how to use 911.
- Go over the security system at least three times. The alarm should be put on when you leave the house.
- Ask a friendly neighbor to keep an eye out.
- There should be no pizza or other deliveries where your child would have to open the door.
- Make it clear who is in charge of younger siblings.
- Tell the child to screen phone calls with the answering machine and speak only to people she knows.

If you absolutley have anxiety attacks when you leave your Tween alone or with younger siblings, then spring for a sitter. The peace of mind will be worth it.

~ 9 ~

Sensitive Issues

There are sensitive issues that every child faces. These issues are amplified by the Tween years. The way you understand and help your child through these often difficult times can keep your child on track and avert dangerous consequences. These turbulent times and how you cope with them can also ultimately establish a closer relationship between you and your Tween.

By the time your child is ten or eleven, don't be surprised if he or she has kissed a boy or girl. Do you remember seven minutes in heaven when you were in sixth grade? It is the discussion about feelings for another person and the meaning of a relationship that are important for you and your Tween. When you do offer advice about boy-girl relationships, don't expect your preteen to greet it with excitement. You'll get a rolling of the eyes and a lot of wincing faces and nervous twitches—but stand firm. This is an important topic.

Yes, Sex!

"You and Dad don't do it, do you Mom?" asked Kim, a budding eleven-year-old. Kim was shocked when her dad made a sexual comment to her mom. The look between her parents somewhat upset Kim. After all, they were her parents. They weren't supposed to have sex.

Adolescents have a difficult time believing that their parents are sexual beings. They would rather subscribe to the stork theory than imagine that Mom and Dad ever had sexual desires—let alone the fact that they "did it." This concept is far too intimate—too personal—for young people to imagine. For this reason, adolescents are often surprised when their parents give advice or explain sexual matters to them.

It is important for children to learn appropriate sexual information from their parents and not from other children or through experimentation. By the time your child is six years old, you should have taught him about the human body, including his sexual organs in nonspecific detail. As your child becomes a Tween, you need to include more detail about sexuality. Often the problem lies in the parent's uneasiness to discuss sex as a natural part of life. Children pick up on their parents' embarrassment and discomfort, and they can interpret this negatively. Your child may get the impression that sex is "bad" or "forbidden." This aura of something being forbidden will give a certain allure to sex. Tweens become preoccupied with the subject and talk about sex incessantly.

Children can learn about sex in inappropriate ways. MTV, their best friend's brother, the movies, and the media can create distorted or inappropriate images for preteens. Sex is often sensationalized on soap operas and talk shows. The subject matter can frighten an impressionable child. Sex and violence are often depicted as synonymous in films and television shows. For these reasons, it is imperative to discuss, by the time your child reaches fifth or sixth grade, the most important issues related to sex: contraceptives and sexually transmitted diseases, especially AIDS. You cannot expect your child's school to teach sex education. Even if the school has a program, it is up to you to make sure all of the information is covered properly. You will also want to follow up with any questions from your preteen.

Here are some things that you can do to help you and your Tween get through the often uncomfortable "sex talk" phase:

- Bring the subject up at a time when you can talk quietly and uninterrupted.
- Have books, videos, and other age-appropriate materials readily available.
- Practice what you want to say ahead of time. Do not laugh or act embarrassed.
- Use simple language that is age-appropriate to your child's maturity level.
- Do not get overly graphic—be straightforward.
- Be positive and infuse your sexual values into the discussion without frightening your child.
- Even if your child says he knows about sex, you should still share your particular views and information.
- Discuss what it means to have a caring relationship with someone of the opposite sex.
- Be prepared to answer some "shocking" questions. Kids will try to catch you off guard. Don't give titillating details.

Whatever you do, try to convey the fact that sex is a pleasant but serious experience between two adults. If you believe a person should be married before having sex, then make that clear. But try to emphasize love, respect, caring, and commitment.

Substance Abuse

Probably the most difficult parenting question you will have to answer is when your preteen asks you, "Did you try drugs?" Most of the Baby Boomer generation "tried" drugs, and many used drugs, often during the turbulent sixties and seventies. But the free-love society is not now—and times and attitudes are drastically different. The answer to your child's question is one that you must answer for yourself. But think through the consequences carefully. They may have a lifelong effect on your child.

Your Tween will be exposed to drugs and alcohol through the media, peers, older siblings of friends, and friends at school. Drugs are in every area of society. Fortunately, schools try to avert substance abuse by instilling anti-use campaigns, but kids get mixed messages. Children see parents drinking alcohol—some even see their parents' widespread use of prescription drugs for everything from weight loss to stress. Drugs are an accepted part of our society.

When Joe went looking for his son Brian's baseball glove, he ended up finding more than he bargained for—a bag of marijuana. Brian was only twelve. Joe lost it. He screamed and yelled and grounded Brian. He demanded to know where on earth Brian had gotten the drugs and how long he'd been smoking marijuana. He wanted to call the police and have the dealer arrested. To Joe's surprise, he learned that many of the kids at school had easy access to not just marijuana but other drugs like cocaine and hallucinogens. Brian made it sound like it was no big deal. He and his wife didn't know where to turn. How could their child from an upper middle class family, who had every advantage, turn to drugs? Part of the problem was his parents' surprise and lack of adequate information.

Danger Signals

Parent awareness of the danger signs of drug use and/or alcohol use is the first step to prevention and necessary intervention. It has been shown in studies that early use of drugs and alcohol can lead to substance abuse. There are danger signals that every parent should be aware of and intervene early and quickly. Many young adolescents think it is "cool" to get involved with drugs or drink alcohol. Kids who are not supervised at parties or at home can get into trouble. Many Tweens want to impress friends and will dare each other to try drugs or drink.

Parents need to

- Find out whose house the party is at
- Determine who is supervising
- Talk with the parents to make sure they will be home
- Set a reasonable curfew
- Remind your child that he or she is to call you immediately if alcohol or drugs are being used, and you will pick him or her up
- Never permit Tweens to "hang out." Ten- to thirteen-year-old children are too young to be hanging out at a mall. Trouble can follow. Poor grades and lack of interest in school or long-range goals can contribute to negative self-esteem.

Children who crave instant gratification may turn to drugs. Since school does not provide "quick highs" for children who are not motivated and reluctant to try, these kids may turn to drugs or alcohol to give them that quick high they desire. Certain children are unable to see how much they can achieve in the future. They take on a "what does it matter" attitude.

Parents need to stay active in their child's life:

- Assist your child with homework.
- Stay in touch with your child's teacher.

- Get involved with the school.
- Get your child involved in sports and after-school activities.
- Look for outside tutoring or counseling if your child has trouble.
- Be aware of any behavioral changes.

If your child falls into an antisocial peer group—kids who are on the fringe, do poorly in school, get into trouble often, spend time in unsupervised activities, and push the societal limits—then your child is more likely to use drugs and drink. Children will emulate their peers and if their peers set a poor example, a child will likely follow.

Your parental task is to make sure you know your child's friends. Talk to the parents, invite his friends over, and engage them in conversation. Observe the child's manners and attitudes. Watch how your child acts in the presence of certain children.

Talk to your Tween often. Provide information and don't be afraid to use graphic examples of what drug and alcohol abuse can do to a person. Let your child know that you are there to help him no matter what he does, and you will give him love, guidance, and help—no questions asked—if he gets into a dangerous situation.

Eating Disorders

Food brings us immeasurable pleasure and untold pain. It has become an American passion. Food no longer represents survival, but is rather the all-consuming subject of talk shows, magazine articles, medical clinics, spas, and conventions—an industry destined to get you healthier and thinner. Unfortunately, our food fanaticism has been embraced by our children. One young girl of nine went on diet after diet to prevent her body from getting "bigger." Even when the doctor told her that she was growing, she saw it as a sign of fat and refused to eat. My friend's eleven-year-old instructs her on the calorie count of every morsel she puts in her mouth. She can recite fat grams with unrivaled accuracy.

Mothers who "starve" themselves thin and obsess over their weight will most likely find their child (usually a daughter) becoming obsessed with weight issues. Because children model our behavior, it is not unusual that ten-year-old Justine has been weighing herself three times a day since she was seven, just like her mother. Justine's mother obsesses about weight. She views herself as "fat" even though she is almost skinny. Justine has been watching and modeling her mother, and thus perceives the same body image.

Conversely, many children who are so frustrated by the relentless push for thinness will go in the opposite direction and eat out-of-control in order to push down feelings. Eating becomes a comfort—a security blanket—with which to deal with chaotic feelings.

Sherri's mother, Dana, spent years telling Sherri all that mattered was to be thin. She would snatch food out of Sherri's hands and chastise her if she gained a few pounds. By seventeen, Sherri had gained a great deal of weight. She was hiding candy bars under her bed.

Food is a highly sensitive issue with preteens. The overemphasis on weight starts at about adolescence. It is more likely girls will develop an eating disorder than boys.

Joyce, mother of twelve-year-old Lisa, was worried when she noticed Lisa was not eating the lunches she made and then picked at her dinner. Lisa was losing weight and appeared gaunt. When Joyce questioned Lisa, the girl admitted that all her friends watch their weight because they don't want to be fat and unpopular. She even showed Joyce pictures in magazines of young models her age. "See, they all are thin!"

Lisa didn't perceive that she was not only thin, but well on her way to becoming anorexic, as many of her friends would become as they entered their teen years.

Beauty or Beast

"Be thin, be beautiful, and be popular." This was the motto of twelve-year-old Tina's mother. But Tina was not thin and beautiful, so she felt worthless because she was unable to live up to her mother's expectations.

The message we give our children about body image and beauty, especially young, impressionable preteens, is a strong one. Your Tween will model your eating behavior. The value you place on being beautiful will imprint your Tween's values. Of course, these subtle and not-so-subtle messages are also fed to your children by the media and advertising executives who set impossible standards for young teens to follow. Almost 40 percent of the articles in magazines focus on appearance. The majority of the models who appear in magazines and on television are underweight, and many are anorexic.

Boys, as well as girls, are plagued by images of perfection. Both genders are prone to abuse food as a way to avoid feelings. The Tween years are an especially vulnerable time because of the numerous physical and psychological changes taking place.

Tweens tend to emulate their peers, and they place a great deal of emphasis on outside role models. Stare at the posters on your child's bedroom wall, and you will quickly see whom she wants to look like. Preteens are a trusting group and believe the media messages they get. The catch comes when your Tween finds she can't reach impossible standards and look like the models in the magazines. She may diet in order to convince herself that if she just loses a few more pounds, she'll be just like the fantasy images she idealizes.

Often, eating disorders in boys are related to feelings. Boys traditionally are "feeling avoiders." They have a more difficult time discussing their emotional lives. A boy may turn to food as a way to push down feelings. Food becomes a comfort. But boys also hear the same message from the media about weight. Male models in magazines and on television are buffed up and perfect visions.

There must be a conscious effort to redirect the emphasis on *thin* and focus on *healthy*. Our society is almost masochistic in its striving to reach unattainable weight goals. Ironically, America has one of the most serious problems with obesity of any other country in the world. This obsession creates anxiety, which causes young people to turn to food as a means of pacifying their anxiety. It is a vicious cycle

Eating Disorders		
Disorder	Signs to Look For	Personality Traits
Anorexia	• Thin • Rigid diet • Exercises obsessively	• Perfectionist • Competitive
Bulimia	• Eating is stress related • Uses bathroom after meals • Diets and binges	• Perfectionist • Competitive

that does not appear to be abating unless parents take an active role in redirecting their Tweens' interests in weight and body image issues.

Anorexia and bulimia are up to epidemic proportions among teen girls. Part of this is due to media exposure and part to female role modeling at home. Many preteens are modeling after weight-conscious mothers who obsess about diets and food. Since parents are the primary role models, children will emulate their behaviors. The following tips will guide you in helping your child and yourself deal with food-related issues.

• Do not talk endlessly about food.
• Make healthy food choices.
• Do not point out and admire overly thin models, actresses, and girls on the street.

- Never tell your child he or she looks "fat."
- Get your child in some sports or exercise program on a regular basis.
- Do not discuss your weight.
- Avoid getting on the scale more than once a day.

Most eating disorder specialists recommend that you teach your child to eat when hungry and stop eating when full.

Don't worry when your daughter gains weight at nine or ten years; a growth spurt prior to entering puberty is normal.

Part of eating disorder problems relates directly to beauty images and what they portray. Eleven-year-old Jody hated herself because she couldn't live with pimples, braces, and her emerging body. She felt ugly and had little self-esteem. Mary Pipher, author of *Reviving Ophelia*, points out that "culture tends to train children what to love and value and what to dislike and devalue. That includes not only what they value external to themselves but also what they value within themselves." Girls and boys start to devalue that which is not pretty and handsome at an early age.

The adage "beauty comes from inside" must be instilled at an early age. Discuss beauty as a concept of change and perception with your child and go over the myths of beauty that follow. Emphasize all of your child's other qualities and make her aware that beauty comes in many colors, sizes, and forms.

The Five Myths of Beauty
(Allana C. Elavson)

1. To be feminine, one must be beautiful.
2. There is only one way to be beautiful.
3. One can be loved, liked, and respected by others if one is beautiful.
4. With the right kind of beauty, one needs little else.
5. Anyone can be beautiful if they put effort into it.

These myths can be broken down by holding up role models who have become successful regardless of how they look.

Depression

"I want to kill myself!" said the thirteen-year-old girl.

Her mother laughed unknowingly. "Don't be ridiculous. You have everything to live for. Now go do your homework."

That night, the thirteen-year-old took enough sleeping pills to land her in the hospital. Her perplexed parents asked, "What did we do wrong? Why would she want to kill herself? We give her everything. Her life is just beginning."

But for this young girl, her life felt like it was over. Nothing her parents said could ease the pain of adolescence. For this child, life was unbearable. Her diagnosis—depression.

Depression is affecting a larger number of young Tweens. Every young adolescent goes through highs and lows, sadness, peer problems, fears, and difficulty with their changing bodies and minds. But depression goes beyond these signposts of adolescence. Parents are often not totally aware of all the pressures preteens face. We see them as young—on the verge of their lives—with myriad opportunities and experiences in front of them. But their perception is often different. Some Tweens idealize their future, but in today's competitive, fast-paced world, it is harder and harder to see endless possibilities. Kids are bombarded with input about drinking, drugs, sex, AIDS, gangs, violence, and issues relating to eating disorders and self-esteem. They become fearful and nontrusting of what they perceive as a hostile world. Tweens who don't have a strong internal psychological base can view life as "not worth living."

It is up to parents to infuse positive images and foster self-esteem and coping skills in their children. It cannot be emphasized enough how important it is to deal with communication and problem-solving skills (see also Chapter 7). These are often the keys to helping a child cope with what *seem* like insurmountable problems.

Of course, sometimes no matter what you do, you may not be able to help your child without outside help. If he or she has signs of chronic depression, it is best to consult a psychologist or psychiatrist. Medication or therapy may be prescribed.

There are many reasons for depression: loss of a loved one, drugs, low self-esteem, alcohol, struggles with emerging and gender identity, and hereditary factors. Don't feel responsible for your child's unhappiness. The key is to try to see the signs early on and get him help. Don't feel responsible for reasons that may be out of your control.

If your Tween seems sad and withdrawn, encourage him to talk—if not to you—to friends. Keep your door and the communication lines open. Parents need to be especially aware that changes in the family, namely divorce, can cause a child to become depressed. You and your ex-spouse need to be a support system for your child and keep his needs a priority.

Many children will say everything is fine but may show other signs of depression like school problems and eating disorders. Look for the signs of depression. No one thing signals depression. Remember, Tweens are a hormonally moody bunch, so don't get panicked over a mood swing. Your child will show a number of these signs (a minimum of three), and they will last for a period of time, not just a day or two.

Signs of Depression

- Lack of appetite over a prolonged period
- Lethargy or being tired all the time
- Crying and feeling sad frequently
- Emotional outbursts over minor issues
- Withdrawal from friends
- Pessimism about the future
- Fearful
- Obsessive thoughts
- Chronic anxiety and panic
- Disinterest in school or grades

When you have identified the signs of depression in your Tween, first seek help through school, your doctor or pediatrician, or the mental health center in your city. Make teen talk lines and other access of communication available to your Tween.

Also, don't negate his feelings. Remember, he needs your support and understanding. No matter how small you may think his problem is, he feels like his world is crashing in.

The following statements are what to avoid saying to your Tween when he appears to be depressed:

What Not to Say to Your Tween If You Suspect He Is Depressed

- What could you possibly be unhappy about?
- My stress is worse than yours.
- You don't know what problems are.
- You shouldn't feel that way.
- Be happy. Everything will look a lot brighter tomorrow.

Depression is not an incurable disease. Do not be afraid to reach out to your child. He wants your guidance, understanding, and love. Find him the help he needs.

There is nothing more enlightening than talking to Tweens and getting their candid opinions. Although certainly not meant to be earth shattering, it can be enlightening (and amusing) to hear preteens talk amongst themselves. They were more than generous to let me into their world for a brief time.

∼ 10 ∼

Tweens Talk

This is an open, unedited dialogue with Tweens about their thoughts, ideas, feelings, and emotions—what they want their parents to know.

A Girl's Perspective

Ten-, eleven-, twelve-, and thirteen-year-old girls talk . . .

Q. What would you like to tell parents about yourself that may be misunderstood?

Roxy: Parents sometimes butt into things that's our own business.

Mara: My mom asks questions about who likes whom. Sometimes I like to share and sometimes

I don't. But she presses me for answers. I would rather not discuss my personal life.

Zoe: When I tell my mom something personal, she tells her friends. When you tell them something private, it should be private. My mom might lecture me about boys if I tell her my feelings, and then she gains control.

Roxy: My mom treats me like I'm a baby, but I have feelings. If I tell her I like so-and-so, she says, "That's so cute!"

Zoe: Parents think we're going to have sex or something. We just want to kiss, dance, and hold hands.

Roxy: When I'm buying clothes and it's the right size, my dad thinks it's too tight. He's overprotective. We like certain styles. We're not trying to be sexy—just in fashion.

Julie: My dad chaperoned a party, and the boys were being wild, and he was so mad. I was embarrassed because he yelled at them. They were just being boys—they didn't destroy anything. They were just acting silly.

Zoe: Yeah. Parents overreact. They think we don't have any sense—like we're gonna act crazy or something. We aren't dumb. We know when someone is doing something really dangerous or bad.

Mara: Yeah! I wish my mom would trust my decisions more. I'm not a baby.

Roxy: Parents think that if you hear a bad word, you'll be bad. We know what's OK—I never swear, but I've heard swear words in movies and on CDs. Like, so what's the big deal?

Julie: Parents are scared cause there is a lot of violence and scary things. I get frightened about a lot of things.

Roxy: Parents scare us too much about violence and kidnappings. They make us so paranoid. My parents seem to worry too much.

Zoe: For sure. I never feel like I'm free—like I could stay alone without a baby-sitter like my mom did when she was young. We have alarms, baby-sitters, mace cans, and a dog.

Jennifer: My parents are too nosy about my private life. They ask too many questions. I don't want them to be concerned, but they still worry too much. Kids my age are different because things are happening earlier now than when she was young. Now there are boy/girl couples in fifth grade.

Zoe: My dad teases me. "Oh, your shirt is too small and too tight."

Jennifer: My parents think that I don't know anything and I'm so childish. Like if a movie comes out like "Addicted to Love," my mom didn't think I should know about sex and love. But at other times my parents think I know too much. It's confusing.

Roxy: I mostly get in fights with my mom about everything. Like we bug each other. She embarrasses me sometimes like yelling at me in front of my friends. If she doesn't like something I'm doing, she'll take me aside and talk or yell at me.

Mara: If I'm on the phone and she wants to use the phone, she'll pick up the receiver and tell me to get off. I hate that. I need my own phone line!

Sometimes she doesn't respect my privacy like if my friend and I want to talk on the speakerphone and she listens. What does she think is so interesting?

My mom shares things about me with her friends and my dad after I've told her not to. That really bugs me.

A new day and a new dialogue . . .

Matty: I argue with my sister a lot. I think boys at this age are *boys*—different—some are shy and stupid. Some are mean.

Roxy: Boys are problem children.

Matty: (giggle) Girls act more grown up, but at my school they are too mature for their age. They wear clothes that are too sexy, and their bras are showing. They wear undershirts to school. It's gross.

Matty: Boys at my school like older girls—a whole year or two older. There are drugs, and parents don't know that they're around.

Kids talk about smoking pot and drugs, and parents think we're too young. I know one boy who was in fifth grade who smoked marijuana at school and got kicked out. His parents defended him. Can you believe it?

Allison: Some boys tease kids and are mean to them. The older kids aren't very nice to us. They think they know it all.

Roxy: Kids disobey rules more at this age. Sometimes I get scared and nervous.

Matty: Me, too, and I don't know why.

Allison: My mom thinks I don't let my feelings out.

Matty: Mine wants me to go talk to a therapist at school.

Allison: They don't understand that our feelings are ours, and we don't need to talk about them all the time. I talk to friends about my feelings.

Q. What's good and bad about your parents?

Zoe: My parents try to understand my feelings sometimes.

Jennifer: I like it when my mom cuddles with me at night, and buys me things.

Julie: My mom is tough on me, but in my heart I know she wants what's best for me. She's just too worried about things. We fight too much, and I get sad.

Mara: My parents think about money too much. Everything is too expensive or too overpriced. But I still want my own phone line!

Roxy: My dad stresses about everything. Mom is worried he'll have a heart attack. It scares me sometimes.

Jennifer: I love my parents most of the time. I mean I'd really be sad if they died. I'd cry forever, especially for my mom.

Matty: Don't even talk about that.

Roxy: My mom has breast cancer. I'm worried she's going to die. But she said she's OK. I think about it a lot.

Jennifer: (teary-eyed) She'll be all right. Don't even worry. My aunt had it, and that was like before I was born, and she's still around.

Allison: Can we change the subject? I'm really getting upset.

A Boy's Perspective

Ten-, eleven-, and twelve-year-old boys talk candidly . . .

Q. What do you want your parents to know about you and your friends?

Ron: Nothing!

Josh: Not to butt into our business.

Ben: My mom asks me a million questions. I hate it. I just don't answer.

Kevin: My dad keeps pushing me to be in sports, and I don't like sports. He is driving me nuts— as if something is wrong with me. I like working on my computer instead.

Ben: All my dad talks about is if I keep playing football as good as I am, I can get a college scholarship. Pressure!

Josh: Yeah—that's another problem. My parents don't trust me. They think I'm going to get in trouble on the Internet. I'm not that dumb. I wouldn't call or give out my number to some stranger or some pervert.

Ron: Have you gotten the AIDS-condom talk yet?
(laughs and some crude language)

Kevin: I'm not even in eighth grade yet, and my dad is worried about AIDS.

Josh: Maybe you should.
(more laughs)

Ben: Yeah—you should worry!
(more laughs)

Josh: The girls barely want to French kiss.

Ron: Well, *some* girls like to do more.

All: Who? Who?
  (more laughs)

Ben: I think girls are cute but stuck up.

Josh: I can't stand girls who act so old and dress like my sister.

Twelve- and thirteen-year-olds—a new day . . .

Michael: I'm thirteen, and my parents think I'm too young to be seriously interested in girls. By fourteen, a lot of guys are doing it with fifteen- and sixteen-year-olds.

Nick: Yeah. That's true. But I'm like really worried about AIDS. My dad has totally made me paranoid.

Michael: Use a condom.

Nick: My dad says they don't always work.

Michael: You're not going to get AIDS from a teenage girl.

Nick: How do you know?

Michael: Get over it.

Nick: You're a sex fanatic ever since you got ahold of your brother's magazines.

Michael: Shut up.

Josh: We don't want to talk too much 'cause our parents will know it's us.

Epilogue

Tweens are terrific—and turbulent and trying. They are the links to childhood and adolescence. They are open and candid and silly and serious. It is difficult to define a Tween because they change from one minute to the next. A Tween will keep you up with the latest, the hippest, and the coolest. You will start to look old to your Tween, and you may start to feel old, too.

My own Tween points out gray hairs on my husband's head, and she lets me know when she thinks my fashion sense is off! The energy you need for the preteen years is enormous. You can no longer pass an issue off. Your child wants thoughtful answers. He will call you on your "stuff" if you try to lie or patronize him. Tweens are smart, savvy, and sophisticated.

If all this sounds like a lot to handle, it is. Parenting is a continuing process that keeps us on our toes—always learning from our children. My twelve-year-old daughter challenges me constantly to be a better parent. The older she gets, the more she reminds me of the lessons that I taught her. It is difficult to break my own rules without her shaking her head. The Tween years are closer to us because they are those awkward, geeky years that every adult remembers vividly. Look at an old yearbook, and your own preteen years will flood back into your memory.

Your Tween's body and mind are expanding in every direction. One minute giggling, the next crying. You may not know what to do or say to help. It was easier when your child was younger. A hug eased his pain. But now you are expected to do more. Hopefully, my book has provided some help and some insight.

It's easier when going through trying times to know that you are not alone—that you have company. Well, you do. There are more parents than can be counted who are struggling with the Tween years—those push, pull, yes, no years that will propel you and your child into a new wonderful time in your lives.

A Final Thought: Trust Yourself

You probably bought this book to learn more about your preteen and to gain new insight into how to communicate and solve problems. After writing six parenting books and interviewing hundreds of parents, my best and final advice is to *trust yourself*.

No one knows or loves your child like you do. You have keen insights into your child's personality. You may periodically need to fine tune your parental transmitter, but I'm sure it works fine.

Trust yourself—your decisions, opinions, and gut instincts. You know intuitively what is the correct way to act, react, and help your child. You know what is right, wrong, decent and indecent. You can recognize good character, kindness, and goodness in a person. You know what it means to be responsible.

You are capable of sharing, fair play, teamwork, and positive thinking. You know what it means to be goal-oriented and driven to do your best.

So trust yourself to pass on all that you know, feel, think, and believe to your Tween, and I am certain that your preteen will grow up to be quite a magnificent adult.

Recommended
Reading

All Grown Up and No Place to Go, by David Elkind. Reading, Mass.: Addison–Wesley, 1998.

Between Parent & Teenager, by Dr. Haim G. Ginott. New York: Avon, 1969.

Get Out of My Life, but First Could You Drive Me and Cheryl to the Mall?, by Anthony E. Wolf. New York: Noonday Press, 1991.

How to Stop the Battle with Your Teenager, by Don Fleming, Ph.D., with Laurel J. Schmidt. New York: Fireside, 1989.

Positive Parenting Your Teens, by Karen Renshaw Joslin and Mary Bunting Decher. Greenwich, Conn.: Fawcett, 1997.

Rebel Without a Car, by Fred Mednick. Minneapolis: Fairview Press, 1996.

Reviving Ophelia, by Mary Pipher, Ph.D. New York: Putnam, 1994.

Uncommon Sense for Parents with Teenagers, by Michael Riera, Ph.D. Berkeley, Calif.: Celestial Arts, 1995.

Venus in Blue Jeans, by Nathalie Bartle, Ed.D., with Susan Lieberman, Ph.D. Boston: Houghton Miflin, 1998.

You and Your Adolescent, by Laurence Steinberg, Ph.D., and Ann Levine. San Francisco: Harper Perennial, 1990.

Index